Discover the Power of Period 9
FENG SHUI and CHINESE ASTROLOGY
2024 - 2044

Your destiny is in your hands. Make the most of it.
Michele Castle

The world is changing rapidly, and if the past few years are any indication, it's not slowing down anytime soon. It is all too human to resist change, to stay in our comfort zone and avoid the great unknown. However, these things don't last. It won't be long before the passage of time irrevocably changes what's familiar to you; that is certain.

But, inevitable as they might be, changes are not always scary and unwelcome. They are an opportunity to challenge the status quo and emerge better than you began. This book seeks to give you the insights and inspiration you need to best prepare for the opportunities and challenges that may come your way.

This book contains a wealth of information from the Feng Shui and Chinese Astrology perspective. Being conscious and aware of what's happening will lead you to the desired outcome. Even in your most uncertain moments, the transition into Period 9 is inevitable. Anticipate what's ahead using these tools, and you will live an inspired life.

Michele

MICHELE CASTLE

Discover the Power of Period 9
FENG SHUI and CHINESE ASTROLOGY
2024 - 2044

PERIOD 9 FENG SHUI AND CHINESE ASTROLOGY

Published by Complete Feng Shui
Mb: 0421 116 799, (+61)
Email: info@completefengshui.com.au
Websites: www.completefengshui.com

Period 9 Feng Shui and Chinese Astrology 2024 - 2044 ©
Text copyright © Michele Castle Illustrations copyright © Michele Castle

All rights reserved. No part of this publication may be reproduced, stored in a retrieval system or transmitted in any form, or by any means, electronic, mechanical, photocopying, recording, or otherwise, without the prior written permission from Complete Feng Shui.

The author's moral right to be identified as the author of this book has been asserted.

Author: Michele Castle
Design copyright @ completefengshui
Title: Period 9 Feng Shui and Chinese Astrology 2024 - 2044

ISBN 978-0-646-88263-5
August 2023

This Book has been written to offer insight and planning for Period 9 Feng Shui (2024-2044) energies for Flying Stars, 8 Mansions, Bagua and Chinese astrology. The author, editor and publisher take no responsibility for the outcome of any information implemented from this Book.

The information in this Book is summarised using Landform, Compass, Flying Star, 8 Mansions, Bagua and Bazi Formulation as per the Chinese Thousand Year Calendar, presented for you in a user-friendly way to help you enjoy prosperity throughout Period 9.

Vice President of the Association of Feng Shui Consultants (AFSC)
Platinum member of the Association of Feng Shui Consultants (AFSC)
Recognised Feng Shui training institution by the (AFSC)

facebook@completefengshui   instagram@completefengshui

Book Cover, Book Layout & eBook Conversion by manuscript2ebook.com

CONTENTS

Introduction to Period 9 Feng Shui 12

Why Michele is so enthusiastic about Feng Shui 14

What is Feng Shui 18

How Does Feng Shui Work? 20

Time Afflictions 29

Your guide to property selection 32

Understanding Feng Shui 40

Understanding the direction and location of your property 43

Terms to know 50

Talking Mountains and Water 66

Understanding the Mountain Impact and Feng Shui 68

Understanding the Water Impact and Feng Shui 74

Feng Shui Basics – The Five Elements 77

Period 9 – The Grand Reset 84

Feng Shui and the Elements – Understanding Period 9 90

Optimising your living space for Period 9 Fulfillment 92

Crucial Sectors for Period 9 94

Refresh - quick property checklist 96

Understanding Life Destiny Palace Gua or Kua 98

Your Gua Numbers 1900 – 2054 102

Meanings of the Directions and Locations 109

Life Palace Destiny number analysis 112

Personal Space selection 121

Personalisation with 8 sectors Bagua 124

Activating the sectors 126

Flying Star Feng Shui for Period 9 128

What you need to do to be able to change the period of building 131

Period 1 Flying Star Chart (1864-1884) 131

Period 2 Flying Star Chart (1884-1904) 138

Period 3 Flying Star Chart (1904-1924) 139

Period 4 Flying Star Chart (1924-1944) 140

Period 5 Flying Star Chart (1944-1964) 141

Period 6 Flying Star Chart (1964-1984) 142

Period 7 Flying Star Chart (1984-2004) 143

Period 8 Flying Star Chart (2004-2024) 144

Period 9 Flying Star Chart (2024-2044) 145

How to get the stars activated 149

Chart activation of Period 9 154

Best Activation for Period 9 Property 158

How to Optimise your Period 8 built property 181

Flying Star Characteristics and Meaning 190

81 Flying Star combination meaning 195

Chinese Astrology in Period 9 225

The Rat (1924, 1936, 1948, 1960, 1972, 1984, 1996, 2008, 2020, 2032) 226

The Ox (1925, 1937, 1949, 1961, 1973, 1985, 1997, 2009, 2021, 2033) 228

The Tiger (1926, 1938, 1950, 1962, 1974, 1986, 1998, 2010, 2022, 2034) 130

The Rabbit (1927, 1939, 1951, 1963, 1975, 1987, 1999, 2011, 2023, 2035) 133

The Dragon (1928, 1940, 1952, 1964, 1976, 1988, 2000, 2012, 2024, 2036) 134

The Snake (1929, 1941, 1953, 1965, 1977, 1989, 2001, 2013, 2025, 2037) 236

The Horse (1930, 1942, 1954, 1966, 1978, 1990, 2002, 2014, 2026, 2038) 238

The Goat (1931, 1943, 1955, 1967, 1979, 1991, 2003, 2015, 2026, 2039) 240

The Monkey (1920, 1932, 1944, 1956, 1968, 1992, 2004, 2016, 2027, 2040) 242

The Rooster (1921, 1933, 1945, 1957, 1969, 1993, 2005, 2017, 2028, 2041) 244

The Dog (1922, 1934, 1946, 1958, 1970, 1994, 2006, 2018, 2029, 2042) 246

The Pig (1923, 1935, 1947, 1959, 1971, 1995, 2007, 2019, 2030, 2043) 248

Career Choices in Period 9 250

Glossary of standard terms and meanings 259

About Michele Castle 307

INTRODUCTION TO PERIOD 9 FENG SHUI:

UNLOCKING THE POWER OF FLYING STARS

Welcome to Period 9 Feng Shui, where ancient wisdom meets modern living. In this book, I will delve into the best way to make the most of Period 9 with the fascinating concept of Feng Shui, your Gua or Life palace and how your Bazi or Four Pillars of Destiny and Flying Stars, will affect you and all its significance in Period 9. Whether you're an avid follower or a beginner seeking to understand this profound practice, this book will guide you through the essentials, providing a rich source of information.

Initially perceived as complex and mathematical, Flying Stars Feng Shui has become more accessible to enthusiasts worldwide. It offers valuable insights into the energetic dynamics of our living spaces, showing us how the flow of energy influences our well-being and success. While it is not astrology or numerology, Flying Stars shares similarities with these practices, using numbers and calculations to determine our environment's auspicious and inauspicious influences.

Period 9, which begins on February 4, 2024, marks a significant milestone in the energy of Flying Stars. This twenty-year cycle brings about transformative changes that impact the luck and fortunes of our homes and buildings. By understanding the principles of Flying Stars, we can proactively safeguard and enhance the energy in our spaces, enabling us to survive and thrive in this critical Period.

This book will explore the unique characteristics and meanings associated with Period 9. The purple and the middle daughter symbolise the number 9 Li Trigram fire star, which radiates energy in all directions. Fire is linked to passion, enthusiasm, and sociability, making it an influential force in this Period. We will witness a growing emphasis on social status and self-image, particularly among middle-aged and younger females. Women's empowerment in various aspects of society will be a notable development during this time.

Understanding the symbolism and attributes of the number 9 Li Fire Star, we gain insights into the industries and professions that will thrive in Period 9. Beauty, aesthetics, artificial intelligence, culture, education, and healthcare will experience significant growth and impact. We will witness technological advancements, media, arts, spirituality, and renewed interest in religious and ethical practices.

As we explore the Flying Stars in Period 9, we discover the auspicious and untimely stars influencing our fortunes. The number 9 star, also known as the Purple King star, brings positive changes to the world, while the number 1 and 2 stars symbolise power and influence. However, we must be mindful of the declining and negative stars, such as the number 5 yellow star, which requires specific cures and enhancers to mitigate its harmful effects.

Period 9 invites us to embrace visibility and adapt to the shifting energies. With the rise of social networks and digital platforms, we must harness the power of media and technology to make our mark in the world. The current global circumstances have accelerated this process, emphasising the importance of our online presence.

In this book, we will equip you with the knowledge and tools to confidently navigate the energies of Period 9. Whether you seek personal harmony or desire to enhance your professional success, understanding and applying the principles of Flying Stars Feng Shui will empower you to create a harmonious and prosperous environment.

WHY MICHELE IS SO ENTHUSIASTIC ABOUT FENG SHUI…

You may ask what led a young mother of three toward such an obscure field. A roller coaster is the perfect description: "Any phenomenon, period, or experience of persistent or violent ups and downs, as one fluctuating between prosperity and recession or elation and despair."

Perth will always be home to me. I was raised by a builder and lived in Belair, Cobar, Bowen, and Echuca. Moving around meant that I experienced many different housing arrangements. I went from the prestigious Belair to a home on stilts that rocked at the front with movement.

One home stood out amongst the lot: the home of my Aunty Nikki. Working in a furniture shop in affluent Subiaco, her home décor was bursting with patterns, fabrics, and textures. I wanted one just like it and aspired to be in Interior Design. I studied the profession, which led to architectural drafting. Fascinated by the impact of design elements on a home, I started analysing my life and the countless houses I had once called home, looking at the shifts in energy and luck in each household.

More than twenty years ago, Feng Shui was brought to my attention as it rapidly gained momentum and interest in the West. Like many, I read about the subject. Friends had their homes healed, and my curiosity flourished. A Feng Shui consultant came to my home with a pen in hand, and I followed her around as she instructed me on colours, furniture placement, and an assortment of symbolism. Red needed to be removed from a wall, and furniture directions required adjustment. Jade and Cumquat plants were placed at doors, mirrors, and pictures re-homed, salt went in certain spots, and even crystals hung to redirect energy. The list went on. The thought of a change in luck stimulated my interest and desire. I was in a tailspin – amazed. This was an exciting new venture, an excellent excuse for an upskill, and unbeknownst to me, a change in my life direction.

I am the Chinese Zodiac animal Rooster, so I needed to understand WHY I could not have a particular red wall, WHY I needed to place salt and crystals in certain pockets, and WHY I was affected by mirrors or artwork symbolism. There were many WHYs, so my Feng Shui journey started. I began reading any books relating to the topic I could get my hands on. Every wall was painted, and furniture textures, colours and placements were altered to follow Feng Shui principles. My home was warm and inviting, with lots of energy and light. It looked and felt great. My sister and friends liked the energy and requested I help them achieve similar outcomes. With that, my journey escalated. I began investing in courses under well-recognised Feng Shui masters. I wanted to understand energy's many levels and influence in Feng Shui: The Art of Placement and Manipulation of Energy. Feng Shui as art just clicked; being mathematical, analytical, and practical, it made sense to me.

I loved my hills home, which taught me much about Feng Shui, energy, and relationships, but that was only the start. Since then, I have successfully navigated the Feng Shui industry for over twenty years, mastering a deep understanding of the multi-layered science of practice.

I have taught Feng Shui, Chinese Astrology, and Metaphysical Studies for Silk Road's Asian Studies at Curtin University and worked extensively with emerging businesses and established enterprises on interiors and renovations. Through many years of practising and consulting, I became the author of "Beginners Feng Shui", "365 Feng Shui Tips Journal", "2022 Year of the Tiger Feng Shui and Chinese Astrology", and "2023 Year of the Rabbit Feng Shui and Chinese Astrology" and a public speaker. Each year, I share my wealth of knowledge and experience with many.

WHAT IS FENG SHUI?

Feng Shui is the ancient art of placement, bringing balance between people and their environment. It originated in China, meaning 'wind and water.' We all experience Feng Shui in our lives, feeling a sense of belonging and harmony within nature. Creating balance and harmony increases peace, security, prosperity, happiness, health, love, and luck.

Feng Shui is a mathematical science practiced worldwide for over a thousand years. Most homes and workspaces lack energy balance, causing a lack of harmony. Classical Feng Shui is the primary solution, but modern cures can help.

In the West, Feng Shui has gained popularity as people realised its positive impact on their homes, relationships, and overall well-being. It works by allowing the flow of energy currents known as Chi, creating a vibrant and positive atmosphere. Blocked energies can lead to negative effects like arguments, sickness, misfortune, and setbacks.

The Five Elements (Fire, Earth, Metal, Water, Wood) govern energy and relate to colour. Correct placement of elements and colours can balance the energy forces in your home.

Negative energy in a home can lead to difficulties, conflicts, and obstacles. Feng Shui helps recognise and counteract these influences, aligning your space to nurture growth and improve circumstances.

Destiny and fortune are influenced by various factors but adhering to Feng Shui precepts can create a harmonious home environment promoting health, wealth, and happiness.

Feng Shui begins with a building reading and can include a personal birth chart for each occupant. Various considerations like object placements, colours, relationships, and auspicious directions play a role in enhancing your home or business.

Your living space greatly impacts your well-being, and Feng Shui can turn it into your greatest ally. Selecting a prosperous and auspicious home is wise, and Feng Shui provides additional benefits such as harmony, health, prosperity, better sleep or studying, and increased opportunities for selling a home.

HOW DOES FENG SHUI WORK?

Feng Shui and symbolism, the art of placement and the study of energy, can benefit many people. The more you understand, the more you can help yourself. However, just because you have, and practice good Feng Shui does not necessarily mean terrible things will not sometimes happen! However, you will be better protected.

Your Chinese astrology and *Bazi*, or "Four Pillars of Destiny" charts, will determine how you perform and are impacted from year to year. Always remember to do the right thing and stay within your values and morals. Let karma take care of the rest.

HOW DO YOU EXPLAIN FENG SHUI IN A SENTENCE

"The Feng Shui system was developed and refined based on elements of astronomy, astrology, geology, mathematics, philosophy, psychology, physics, and divination (intuition)."

Three factors make an impact on your life. These factors are:

- Heaven Luck,
- Man Luck; and
- Earth Luck.

Words of wisdom from a grandmaster:

An old wise man said:

"Heaven luck is the boat given to you by God.

Earth luck is the wind that fills the sails and the currents of the ocean.

Human luck is the way in which you use the wind and the currents to steer your boat."

Meaning:

Heaven luck is your destiny, Earth luck is Feng Shui to smooth the path that brings opportunities, and Human luck is "You" and how you can shape your path, destiny, and make use of your opportunities.

These are the components of the cosmic Trinity of Luck.

Your life is always influenced by these three factors. Understanding and mastering the aspects and influences within your environment can have a profound impact on how your influence and performance from one year to the next.

Heaven Luck is the hand you are dealt. It is what is given to you, not by your choosing, but by the energies and forces beyond your control from your date of birth. This is your Bazi or Four Pillars of Destiny chart.

Man, Luck is classified as FREE will and the conscious decisions you make. This includes how you spend your time and which improvements you choose to make in your life. Knowledge, influence, and education empower you to strengthen your man luck and abilities.

Earth Luck is the modern science and our environment. It includes the people we hang out with, or the buildings in which we live or work from. These would be classed as Feng Shui influences.

Based on the cosmic trinity, you can blueprint your life and year ahead by paying special attention to your Man Luck, the aspects and influences in your life and environment; Heaven Luck, the element and animal forecast from your *Bazi*, or Four Pillars of Destiny chart, understand your capabilities, strengths, weaknesses and opportunities; and Earth luck, the Feng Shui or flying stars of your home, environment, and the world around you.

The next element is understanding timing and the significant impact it has on our results/aspirations and ACTION. Simply put, "FATE is when the girl of your dreams walks into the room. DESTINY is whether you decide to approach her or not." Your life and choices are always about the actions you take or do not.

The wonderful thing about Feng Shui is the positive benefits it can create for everyone. Feng Shui is not just about becoming wealthy or achieving success – it is concerned with enriching lives, reducing aggravations, and bringing happiness into relationships. It is about feeling happy, prosperous, and contented.

When you know how to orient your doors, organise the layout of rooms, arrange furniture, incorporate the use of colours, shapes, and materials, and know about the placement of decorative items in your home, you will discover a new energy and zest for life. Life will become joyous and your relationships with loved ones will reach a stronger level of understanding. Interactions with others living in the home will begin to improve too!

If you also know how to keep your Feng Shui up to date from year to year, the benefits will be even greater. When your home exhibits good Feng Shui, it literally becomes infused with harmonious energy and an atmosphere of general health. Your home, now happy and calm, will become a real haven – just as a home should be!

Feng Shui is easily applied. The main rule is to keep the Chi (life force energy) moving – never let it stagnate or become unbalanced. Sound, activity, movement, and people all keep Chi in motion. When a space stays too still and is neglected for a period, it stops. However, the simple act of moving the furniture and using different areas of your home will shift the energy, making you feel much better.

The arrangement of our home space is something many of us take for granted. Often, we focus our attention purely on the aesthetic of arrangement and décor. Insufficient consideration is given to Feng Shui design implications. Correct Feng Shui inputs can improve the luck of almost every home, irrespective of style or decoration.

At worst, bad Feng Shui and negative elements lead to anger, loss, and even violence. Bad Feng Shui means negatives are present, causing many problems such as health issues and monetary loss. If the cause of bad energy is not addressed, you will continue to suffer challenging times.

TIME AFFLICTIONS

The other aspect of Feng Shui that must be accounted for is time. While *physical afflictions* are the result of placement (design, blockages, and orientation), *time afflictions* are caused by the passing of time. Therefore, we have two dimensions that influence Feng Shui: space and time. To ensure that you make the best of *time energy*, you need to update your Feng Shui in accordance with changing time.

The Chinese place great emphasis on the calendar. The main Chinese calendar is the lunar calendar. Each cycle of calendar time is expressed in terms of the Five Elements: Fire, Earth, Metal, Water and Wood. These Five Elements, combined with the twelve animals, make a major cycle that lasts for sixty years.

As we move from one year to the next, energy changes, transforming from Yin to Yang, from element to element, and from one animal sign to the next. Depending on the ruling element and animal from one month to the next, the energy in the home and its resident's change. Time exerts a very strong impact on your Feng Shui, luck, and destiny.

Good Feng Shui cannot and does not last forever. It must be recharged with small but significant changes every year. Energy must be refreshed, reorganised, and rejuvenated; spaces and places need maintenance and energy must keep moving.

The Flying Stars formula of Feng Shui is a technical approach that directly addresses the effect of time on the energy of homes and businesses.

You can tell from month to month where illness energy lingers. This can be suppressed with remedies. Most importantly, you can stop monetary loss, broken relationships, frustration, disharmony, and the pernicious effect of aggravating people with the correct application of cures and enhancers.

By investing the time and effort of Feng Shui in your home, you will have added a valuable resource to your life. After enhancing the energy of your surroundings with Feng Shui, your view and approach to living spaces will never be the same again.

With the understanding of Feng Shui, you can develop an increased sensitivity to the environment around you, with this awareness will come respect for your surroundings. You do not have to "believe" in Feng Shui for it to work, Feng Shui is always all around you…

YOUR GUIDE TO PROPERTY SELECTION

As Feng Shui plays a vital role in creating a harmonious home or apartment. By considering factors like property orientation, surroundings, and layout, one can choose a space that supports health, prosperity, and happiness. Understanding Feng Shui fundamentals helps find a property aligned with personal energy, fostering growth and harmony. Let's look at some tips for pre property purchase.

BEFORE YOU BUY

ASSESSING LAND QUALITY

Assessing land quality before purchasing a building is crucial for long-term luck and investment. Evaluating the soil and land is vital, avoiding poor indicators like tree remnants, metal, sharp boulders, black peat, or buried plastic items. Digging a hole in the land's center reveals its auspiciousness: uncovered indicates financial difficulties, adequately covered denotes average luck, and excess earth forming a mound signifies success. Further, digging a larger hole in the southeast corner determines wealth potential, with water presence indicating natural wealth.

Compact soil and residing in valleys offer greater prosperity potential. Evaluating land quality is simple yet essential for future success.

HOME DESIGN CONCEPTS TO CONSIDER

When it comes to essential home design concepts, there are several key elements to consider. Begin by exploring room images to gather inspiration and set the desired ambiance. Understanding the impact of colours and various light sources is crucial in creating the right atmosphere. Incorporating the sky and skylights can introduce dynamic lighting variations throughout the day, especially if you lack a river, ocean, or valley view. Internal gardens or courtyards serve as captivating central features, while glass screens can provide both privacy and a sense of connection. Look for unique elements within visual planes and surfaces to add interest and character to your space. Employing illusions with materials and structural elements challenges perceptions, fostering intrigue and uniqueness. Ultimately, aim to create a lasting impression through thoughtful cohesive design.

Lastly when buying a new home, it's important to consider Feng Shui principles for a harmonious living environment. Some guidelines to ensure good Feng Shui for purchasing:

Trust your instincts during the viewing process.

Use your compass, mobile phone or Google Earth to assess the property's facing direction and surroundings. (Refer to page 43 on how to take a compass reading.)

Check the home's history, addressing divorce, deaths, and conflicts if necessary.

Evaluate the financial and emotional history of previous occupants.

Observe the neighbourhood's landscaping, animals, and weather changes.

TIPS TO CONSIDER FOR SELECTING A HOUSE

Avoid a house:

1. Situated at the end of a road.
2. Front door facing a cross, T and Y junction or a "no entry" sign.
3. Facing a building or structure with sharp edges.
4. Facing a U-shaped Road.
5. With a main door facing an uphill slope.
6. With a main door facing a temple or religious building.
7. With a main door facing an overpass.
8. That is surrounded by drains.
9. That is surrounded by tall buildings.
10. With the kitchen or toilets in the center and northwest of the house.
11. Situated close to a cemetery.

TIPS FOR SELECTING AN APARTMENT

Avoid an apartment:

1. With an irregular shape unit or with missing corners.
2. With overhead beams near the main door.
3. With a kitchen door facing the main door.
4. With a toilet facing the main door.
5. With a main door facing a flight of stairs.
6. With a main door facing a refuge center or refuge disposal.
7. With a main door facing a pillar or sharp edge.
8. With main door facing a long narrow' corridor/passageway.
9. With a bedroom door facing the main door.
10. With too many sharp edges, pillars or beams.
11. Situated close to a cemetery.
12. Building that faces a temple or religious building.

Take a compass reading to assess Feng Shui suitability based on your destiny number (see page 98 for your destiny number). Consider seeking a professional Feng Shui consultation when necessary.

Adhere to Period 9 Feng Shui fulfillment as per page 94-96

UNDERSTANDING FENG SHUI

Before you dive into implications of Period 9 it is important to understand some of the basics of Feng Shui.

In our lives, we are influenced by both Internal and External Factors, which play a role in shaping our outcomes. Internal Factors relate to our inherent personality and characteristics, which can be determined through our Destiny Code called Four Pillars of Destiny or Bazi. On the other hand, external factors, encompass events, circumstances, or opportunities that come our way without our control, as well as the physical forms in our environment, such as pylons, that can compound issues related to specific areas in our home. By correctly applying Feng Shui, we can alleviate or minimise the effects of these factors.

When we combine Internal and External Factors, we can leverage our strengths and seek an environment that allows us to shine while encountering minimal resistance. This powerful combination of self-improvement and informed decision-making leads to a more fulfilling life.

Classical Feng Shui is an ancient and respected science that explores how cosmic energies, known as Chi, can be harnessed to benefit our internal and external environments. While Chi is intangible, its effects permeate nearly every aspect of our lives, making it the core focus of Chinese Metaphysics.

Classical Feng Shui is centred around the study of Yin and Yang, with its origins in the study of Heaven and Earth. Over time, sophisticated methods were developed during the Tang Dynasty (618-907 AD). Essential factors of Location, Direction, and Time are needed to be understood to be able to define Classical Feng Shui.

Chi a word for energy, constantly circulates within and around us and the environment we live in. As Chi is cyclical, allowing us to study, document, and anticipate its patterns of change. As these patterns shift continuously, it is vital to identify the positive and negative Chi in each direction so that you can plan accordingly. Just as there are positive and negative charges, protons, and electrons in physics, Chi can also have positive and negative qualities.

It is said that "change is the only constant in life".

The Five Arts encompass Mountain, Medicine, Divination, Destiny, and Physiognomy, with Classical Feng Shui falling under the study of land physiognomy (in simple terms the "appearance of the landscape"). It provides us with the knowledge of how to utilise the prevalent Chi to improve our living conditions, our lives, the lives of our loved ones, and ultimately benefit humanity. When properly applied, Classical Feng Shui has proven to be a powerful tool for improvement.

Feng Shui focuses on Landforms and environmental features. It is the science of harnessing the cosmic and natural energies, known as Chi, in our environment to assist us in various aspects of life. Feng Shui can also be used for predictive purposes without any religious or superstitious affiliations.

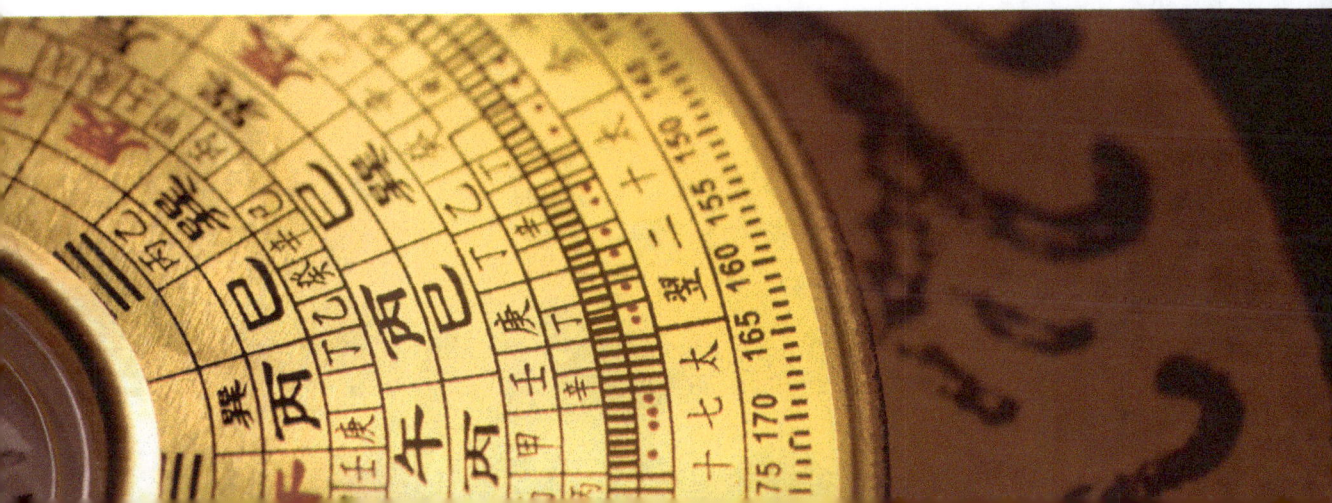

THE FOUR IMPORTANT FACTORS IN FENG SHUI

1. **Environment:**
   The environment in which a property is situated plays a crucial role in influencing the types of Chi present and, consequently, the inhabitants' performance and success in life. Features like mountains, lakes, rivers, roads, and highways circulate and conduct Chi. Understanding which Chi augurs well for specific endeavours and which Chi can negatively affect our quality of life is important. When the environment is conducive to Feng Shui principles, people tend to perform better and lead more fulfilling lives.

2. **Building**
   Every property, whether it's a home or a business, is unique. To assess its Feng Shui, you consider the property's Natal Chart based on its occupancy start time and facing direction. Location, direction, and time are key factors in determining a property's Feng Shui viability.

3. **Residents**
   In Feng Shui, everyone is represented by a personal Life Destiny Palace called a Gua or Kua. This is calculated using birth date and gender, revealing favourable and unfavourable directions. Understanding your personal palace helps you navigate various aspects of life.

4. **Time**
   Time is crucial in classical Feng Shui. Life is constantly changing, and no property or individual experiences continuous good or bad fortune throughout. Assessing Feng Shui involves considering the factor of time.

UNDERSTANDING THE DIRECTION AND LOCATION OF YOUR PROPERTY

First step determining direction and location.

In Classical Feng Shui, direction and location are vital factors. Before applying any Feng Shui system, it's important to determine the correct direction. You will need a compass or your mobile phone.

COMPASS READING AND CARE

HOW TO CARE FOR YOUR COMPASS

Most compasses are quite sturdy, however, there are some things to be mindful of:

- Never put it near a magnet, this can damage the compass and render it useless.
- Do not shake it, as that may dislodge the needle from its pin.
- Use a case or the bag that has been provided to protect your compass.

THE DON'TS OF TAKING A COMPASS READING

There are many things that can alter a compass reading, which may result in getting an incorrect reading:

- Do not take a compass reading near a motor vehicle of any kind.
- Do not take a compass reading near anything metal; be mindful of belt buckles, mobile phones, metal pens in your hand or pockets as these will alter a reading.
- Do not take a compass reading near anything electrical, especially power poles.
- Do not take a compass reading standing on pebbles, pea gravel, iron ore or marble.

THE DO'S OF TAKING A COMPASS READING

To take your reading for Eight Mansions or Bagua*:

1. Stand just outside of your home or business, in front of the building and face the building.
2. Lay your compass flat in one hand.
3. Have the long part of the (base) section pointing away from you and the compass section closest to you.

4. Make sure that the compass is straight.
5. Wait for the needle to settle.
6. Turn the cover until the point of the needle is right in between the two lines (North).
7. Your compass reading (in degrees) is where the middle line that runs under the compass is pointing into the degrees (black print within the circle of the compass) closest to you.

*You will need this information for working out the Flying Star direction of your home or building for Flying Star and Bagua School of Feng Shui.

HOW TO DETERMINE YOUR DIRECTION.

First step, stand outside the door, about one or two feet away.

DOOR FACING VS. BUILDING FACING

Door facing refers to the direction a door or main door faces, while building facing establishes the property's North-South axis. The building's facing direction is based on its intentional architectural frontage.

DETERMINE THE FACADE (BUILDING DIRECTION) OF A PROPERTY.

1. Stand at the middle of the facade facing outward.
2. Use a compass or mobile phone with the needle pointing North to determine the direction you and the house are facing.

DETERMINING THE FACING DIRECTION OF A DOOR

1. Stand about one foot outside the door facing outward.
2. Align the square base of your mobile phone parallel to the door, using the North-South axis on the compass to determine the door's facing direction.

DIRECTION VS. LOCATION

In Feng Shui, direction refers to the angle or perspective a person or object faces, while location represents the spot or place where someone or something is situated. Differentiating between direction and location is important in understanding Feng Shui concepts.

THE COSMIC TRINITY

Before delving into Feng Shui, let's take another look at understanding the Cosmic Trinity is essential. It consists of Heaven Luck (predetermined at birth), Man Luck (our choices and actions), and Earth Luck (the influence of our environment). Classical Feng Shui utilises Earth Luck to optimise your destiny.

WHAT FENG SHUI CAN OR CANNOT DO FOR YOU?

Feng Shui represents Earth Luck, but it's only one component of overall success. Attaining maximum success requires a balance of Heaven Luck, Man Luck, and Earth Luck. Feng Shui cannot help unrealistic expectations or solve problems overnight. It enhances aspects of life but requires effort, self-awareness, and realistic expectations.

HOW CAN FENG SHUI WORK FOR YOU?

Feng Shui works by understanding and facilitating the flow of positive Chi (energy) within a property while mitigating negative Chi. Natural landforms and man-made features influence the type of Chi present. Classical Feng Shui takes time to manifest its effects.

THE THREE (3) CYCLES

The interactions between the Five Elements (Fire, Earth, Metal, Water and Wood) are depicted in the Productive, Controlling, and Weakening Cycles. These cycles illustrate how elements support, balance, or weaken each other. Understanding these cycles helps grasp Feng Shui concepts and achieve balance in life.

TERMS TO KNOW

Before beginning your journey into Feng Shui and Period 9 it is worth understanding some of the common terms and references which will be referred to throughout this book.

NATAL CHART

Natal Star Charts are unique energy maps for structures based on their specific compass direction. Like astrological charts, these charts identify strong and weak aspects, revealing the building's potential. By understanding and activating different sectors with auspicious energy, one can harness the power of Feng Shui.

Feng Shui involves skillfully analysing, correcting, and enhancing energies as they change over time. Flying Stars, a component of Feng Shui, evaluates the invisible life forces that influence the environment and structures, impacting the people who reside or work there.

FLYING STARS

What are the "Stars" in Feng Shui? These "stars" are not celestial bodies in the sky, but rather numerical representations from 1 to 9 that symbolise energy. They serve the purpose of assessing the energy quality within a building. Unlike other systems that focus on the human aspect, such as Eight Mansions and Bagua, these "stars" carry unique qualities and energies that can influence various aspects of life, such as wealth, health, romance, education, writing, fame, and divorce, among others.

Although the "stars" are not actual planets, they have a connection to the seven real stars of the Big Dipper (also known as the Northern Ladle) in Chinese culture, with two additional imaginary stars. The Chinese, like many ancient civilisations, were keen observers of the sky and possessed an advanced understanding of time based on planetary movements.

Time Cycles in Flying Stars Feng Shui are essential for understanding the system in modern-day practice. The Flying Star system incorporates significant time cycles and planetary alignments. There are three key time blocks: the 180-year Great Cycle, three 60-year cycles, and nine 20-year increments known as "Periods.".

TIME CYCLES OF FLYING STAR FENG SHUI

The Great Cycle, also known as the Mega Cycle, is based on the alignment of planets in our Solar System, occurring approximately once every 179 to 180 years. The ancient Chinese scholars first observed this phenomenon around 2500 BC. They further divided the 180-year cycle into three sixty-year cycles: Upper, Middle, and Lower.

Each sixty-year cycle was then subdivided into 20-year Periods or Ages. Each Period is assigned a number from 1 to 9, along with a unique energy-expressing trigram (except for the number 5, which has no trigram). These Periods influence the world's energy for 20 years. The choice of 20-year Periods is interestingly connected to the observation that the Milky Way shifts every 20 years, impacting the fortunes of buildings, homes, and individuals.

THE 24 MOUNTAINS

In both Classical Feng Shui and Flying Stars, the 360-degree compass is divided into 24 sections or directions, each spanning 15 degrees. This division is known as the 24 Mountains and is widely recognised. It means that every abode or building can only face one of these 24 directions. It's important to note that the term "24 Mountains" doesn't refer to literal mountains, but rather serves as a descriptive label.

Each of these 24 directions is further divided into subsectors, with three subsectors assigned to each main direction. For instance, South 1, South 2, and South 3 encompass the entire 45 degrees of the South direction. This subdivision allows for a more precise analysis and application of Feng Shui principles within each subsector.

SUB SECTORS

The subsectors within the 24 Mountain ring in Feng Shui hold significant meaning and play a crucial role in analysing and harnessing the energy of a space. These subsectors are the smaller divisions within each main direction, further refining the Feng Shui analysis. They allow practitioners to assess the energy flow with greater precision and make specific adjustments tailored to each subsector.

By delving into the subsectors, practitioners gain a deeper understanding of the nuances and variations within a particular direction. Each subsector carries its own unique energy qualities, influences, and potential effects on the occupants of a space. This knowledge enables Feng Shui experts to apply targeted remedies and enhancements to optimise the flow of beneficial energy and mitigate any negative influences within specific subsectors.

For example, within a larger direction such as North, there may be subsectors identified as North 1, North 2, and North 3. Each of these subsectors represents a distinct portion of the North direction, allowing practitioners to assess the energy characteristics and recommend appropriate adjustments for that specific area.

Understanding the subsectors of the 24 Mountain ring empowers practitioners to fine-tune their Feng Shui recommendations based on the precise location and orientation of a building. It enhances the accuracy and effectiveness of Feng Shui applications, ensuring that the energy flow is harmonised and optimised

throughout the space, leading to positive outcomes and improved well-being for the occupants.

Facing Star Also known as water stars, these numbers are in the upper right-hand corner in all nine palaces of the chart.

Mountain Star Also known as sitting stars, these numbers are in the upper left-hand corner in all nine palaces of the chart.

Time Star Also known as the base star, this number indicates the Period to which the chart belongs. It is the single star below the facing and mountain stars.

FACING STAR OFTEN REFERED TO AS WATER STAR

The "facing star" is a fundamental concept in Feng Shui that holds profound meaning and influences the energy dynamics of a space. In Feng Shui, each of the eight main compass directions is associated with a specific star, known as the facing star. These facing stars represent distinct energetic qualities and influences, such as wealth, health, relationships, or career.

The facing star determines the primary energy that enters a building or a specific area within it. By understanding and activating the favourable facing star, one can enhance the corresponding aspect of life and attract positive outcomes. On the other hand, if an unfavourable facing star is prominent, appropriate adjustments and remedies can be applied to minimise its negative impact.

The facing star plays a pivotal role in determining the energetic blueprint of a space and guides the placement of key elements, such as entrances, bedrooms, or workspaces, to align with the desired energies. It is crucial to align the facing star with the intended purpose or desired outcome to optimise the flow of beneficial energy and create a harmonious environment.

In summary, the facing star in Feng Shui signifies the primary energetic influence associated with each compass direction. By understanding and activating the appropriate facing star, one can harness the desired energies and create a supportive environment that promotes well-being, prosperity, and harmony.

So, What DO Facing / Water Star's governs … generally, money but, Facing and Water stars also have various meanings and influences.

Wealth and Abundance: Water stars can symbolise wealth and abundance, attracting financial prosperity and opportunities.

Career and Success: Water stars are believed to enhance career luck, promoting success, recognition, and advancement in one's profession.

Communication and Networking: Water stars are associated with effective communication, networking, and building positive relationships with others.

Mental Clarity and Wisdom: Water stars can bring clarity of mind, mental focus, and wisdom, supporting intellectual pursuits and decision-making.

Emotional Balance and Harmony: Water stars are connected to emotional balance, serenity, and harmonious relationships, fostering peace and tranquillity in the home or workspace.

Intuition and Spirituality: Water stars can enhance intuition and spiritual growth, promoting a deeper connection with oneself and the spiritual realm.

Healing and Renewal: Water stars are associated with healing energy, promoting physical, emotional, and spiritual well-being.

It's important to note that the interpretation and influence of water stars can vary depending on their specific placement and combination with other stars or elements in a Feng Shui chart or analysis.

SITTING STAR OFTEN REFFERED TO AS MOUNTAIN STAR

The "sitting star" is a significant concept in Feng Shui that holds profound meaning and influences the energy dynamics of a space. In Feng Shui, the sitting star represents the energetic quality associated with the direction opposite to the facing star. It symbolises the supporting energy that nurtures and provides stability to a building or a specific area within it.

The sitting star determines the foundation and grounding energy of a space, influencing factors such as stability, protection, and overall well-being. It represents the support system that enhances the occupants' ability to thrive and succeed in their endeavours. Activating and harmonising the sitting star is essential to create a balanced and harmonious environment.

Just as the facing star guides the placement of key elements, the sitting star influences the arrangement of furniture, structures, and features within a space. By aligning these elements with the favourable sitting star, one can enhance the supportive energies and create a solid foundation for success and fulfillment.

Understanding the significance of the sitting star allows Feng Shui practitioners to optimise the flow of energy and create spaces that nurture and support the inhabitants' goals and aspirations. By harnessing the power of the sitting star, one can create a harmonious environment that promotes stability, protection, and overall well-being.

In summary, the sitting star in Feng Shui represents the supporting energy associated with the direction opposite to the facing star. It influences stability, protection, and overall well-being, providing a solid foundation for success and fulfillment. By aligning with the favourable sitting star, one can optimise the energetic flow and create a harmonious space that supports and nurtures the occupants' goals and aspirations.

So, What DO Sitting / Mountain Star's governs ... generally, people but, Sitting and Mountain stars also have various meanings and influences.

Stability and Support: Mountain stars represent stability, grounding, and a solid foundation. They provide support and strength to individuals and properties.

Protection and Security: Mountain stars are associated with protection, creating a sense of security, and shielding against negative energies or external influences.

Wisdom and Knowledge: Mountain stars symbolise wisdom, knowledge, and personal growth. They promote intellectual pursuits and encourage continuous learning.

Health and Vitality: Mountain stars are believed to have a positive impact on physical health and vitality, enhancing overall well-being.

Authority and Leadership: Mountain stars signify authority, leadership, and ambition. They support individuals in positions of power or those aspiring to achieve success and influence.

Relationships and Harmony: Mountain stars foster harmonious relationships, both in personal and professional spheres. They promote cooperation, understanding, and balance.

Spiritual Connection: Mountain stars are associated with spiritual connection and inner strength. They encourage introspection, mindfulness, and a deeper connection with oneself.

It's important to note that the interpretation and influence of Mountain Stars can vary depending on their specific placement and combination with other stars or elements in a Feng Shui chart or analysis.

BASE STAR

In the realm of Feng Shui, the "base star" holds a profound significance as a foundational force that influences the energetic essence of a space. Also known as the "mountain star" or "earthly star," the base star represents the underlying energy associated with the specific compass direction of a building or a particular area within it. It symbolises stability, grounding, and the fundamental support upon which the entire Feng Shui system is built.

The base star acts as a solid bedrock, anchoring the flow of energy and providing a sense of rootedness and security. It represents the nurturing energy of the

earth, establishing a solid foundation for the occupants' well-being and success. By understanding and activating the favourable base star, one can tap into its supportive energy and create a harmonious environment that promotes stability, prosperity, and abundance.

The alignment and activation of the base star are crucial in Feng Shui practice, as it determines the auspicious positioning of key elements and features within a space. By harmonising the energy of the base star with the other stars and forces at play, one can optimise the flow of Chi (energy) and create a space that supports personal growth, harmonious relationships, and overall vitality.

The base star is not only associated with physical structures but also influences the energetic landscape surrounding a building. It influences the selection of auspicious locations for important features such as entrances, bedrooms, and workspaces. By honouring and enhancing the energy of the base star, one can create a solid foundation that fosters a harmonious and prosperous living or working environment.

To summarise, the base star in Feng Shui represents the foundational energy associated with the specific compass direction of a space. It symbolises stability, grounding, and fundamental support. By aligning with and activating the favourable base star, one can establish a solid foundation that promotes stability, prosperity, and overall well-being. Understanding and honouring the base star is key to optimising the flow of energy and creating a harmonious environment that nurtures personal growth and success.

ANNUAL MONTHLY STARS

The Flying Stars system not only reveals the energy map of a home or business but also provides valuable insights into the changing energy patterns on an annual and monthly basis. Understanding these shifts is crucial to maintaining continual good fortune. While annual stars do not signify major shifts like transitioning between Periods, they hold significance as they can greatly impact daily events and overall luck. Monthly stars, though less significant, should also be considered. It's important to note that neither the monthly nor annual stars hold the same importance as the natal Flying Star Chart. The purpose of these stars is to alert you to potentially troublesome energy and highlight areas where additional prosperity may manifest throughout the year. By identifying these influences, you can take proactive measures to mitigate negative effects and enhance positive energies in your space.

64 HEXAGRAMS

The "64 Hexagrams" hold great significance in Feng Shui, representing a profound system of divination and wisdom derived from the ancient Chinese classic text known as the I Ching or Book of Changes. These hexagrams are composed of six stacked lines, each line representing Yin or Yang energy. Each hexagram embodies a unique combination of these energies, symbolising various aspects of life, nature, and human experiences. In Feng Shui, the 64 Hexagrams serve as a rich source of knowledge and guidance, offering insights into the dynamic interplay of energies and the patterns of change within the environment. They provide valuable wisdom for understanding the balance, harmony, and transformation in one's surroundings, and can be consulted to gain deeper insights and make informed decisions when applying Feng Shui principles.

LUO SHU

The Luo Shu, also known as the Magic Square or Lo Shu Square, holds significant meaning in Feng Shui. It is a grid consisting of nine squares, each containing a number from 1 to 9. This ancient Chinese divination tool serves as a powerful symbol of cosmic order and balance. The arrangement of numbers in the Luo Shu Square is believed to represent the fundamental principles of the universe. Each number carries its own energy and symbolism, influencing various aspects of life such as wealth, health, relationships, and success. Practitioners of Feng Shui use the Luo Shu to analyse and harmonise the energy flow within a space, aligning it with the favourable forces of nature and promoting harmony and abundance. By understanding the profound wisdom encoded in the Luo Shu, one can unlock the secrets of energy manipulation and create a harmonious and auspicious environment.

HE TU

The He Tu, also known as the River Map, is a fundamental concept in Feng Shui that represents the primal forces of creation and transformation. It is a diagram composed of nine squares, each containing a combination of yin and yang lines. The He Tu embodies the dynamic interplay between the opposing yet complementary forces of nature. It serves as a guide to understanding the flow of energy and the patterns of change within a space. Each square in the He Tu corresponds to a specific element, direction, and aspect of life. By studying the arrangement of the lines and elements in the He Tu, Feng Shui practitioners gain insights into the energetic qualities of a location and can adjust and enhance the flow of positive energy. The He Tu is a powerful tool for balancing and harmonising the energy of a space, enabling individuals to tap into the transformative power of nature and create environments that support growth, prosperity, and well-being.

BA GUA

The Ba gua, also known as the Eight Trigrams, is a foundational concept in Feng Shui that represents the fundamental energies and principles of the universe. It is a symbolic diagram consisting of eight trigrams, each composed of three lines, either broken (yin) or unbroken (yang). The Ba gua serves as a tool for analysing and harmonising the energy of a space, as well as understanding the various aspects of life. Each trigram corresponds to a specific element, direction, colour, and symbolic representation, encompassing areas such as career, relationships, wealth, health, and more. By overlaying the Ba gua onto a floor plan or a specific area, practitioners can assess the energetic qualities and adjust optimise the flow of energy and promote harmony and balance. The Ba gua is a versatile and comprehensive system that provides insights into the interplay between energy and environment, guiding individuals in creating spaces that support their goals and well-being.

EIGHT MANSIONS

The Eight Mansions, also known as the Eight House Feng Shui, is a traditional system in Feng Shui that focuses on analysing and harmonising the energy of a space based on its orientation and the personal energy of its occupants. It classifies individuals into one of eight directions (N, S, E, W, NE, NW, SE, SW) based on their birth year and gender. Each direction is associated with specific energy characteristics and favourable or unfavourable influences. By aligning the

individual's favourable direction with the orientation of their living or working space. The Eight Mansions system aims to enhance their well-being, relationships, career, and overall success. This approach involves adjusting the layout and arrangement of furniture, identifying auspicious areas for important activities, and minimising the impact of unfavourable energies. The Eight Mansions system provides a personalised approach to Feng Shui, considering the unique energy patterns of individuals and their living environments to create a supportive and harmonious atmosphere.

LIFE DESTINY PALACE GUA OR KUA

The Life Destiny Palace Gua, also known as Life Gua or Kua, is a fundamental concept in Feng Shui that determines an individual's auspicious directions and personal energy based on their birthdate. It is calculated using the Chinese lunar calendar and involves identifying one's year of birth and gender. The Life Destiny Palace Gua represents an individual's inherent qualities, strengths, and challenges, and provides insights into their compatibility with certain directions and elements. By understanding their Life Destiny Palace Gua, individuals can align themselves with favourable energies, make informed decisions regarding their living or working space, and enhance various aspects of their life, including health, relationships, career, and personal growth. The Life Destiny Palace Gua serves as a valuable tool in Feng Shui, helping individuals optimise their living environments and harness the supportive energies that resonate with their unique life path and aspirations.

TALKING MOUNTAINS AND WATER

KEY FACTORS IN FENG SHUI – EXTERNAL AND INTERNAL FACTORS

Feng Shui is the study of the Earth's energy and how it is influenced by the land. It focuses on the circulation and qualities of this energy, known as Chi. When applying Feng Shui to a property, it is important to consider the external and internal factors that affect the flow of Chi.

External factors include mountains, water, and the main door. Mountains can produce positive or negative Chi depending on their appearance, with lush green mountains being favourable. Water, such as rivers and lakes, acts as a conductor of Chi. It is important to assess the type and location of water formations to avoid negative Chi. The main door should have a clear and unobstructed space outside and inside, while avoiding negative features like lampposts.

Internal factors that require attention are the main door, kitchen, and bedroom. The main door serves as the entry point for Chi into the house, so its location and direction are crucial. The kitchen should be free from negative external forms and the stove should be properly positioned, avoiding alignment with the kitchen door and being in the centre. The bedroom, being a Yin place, should not have excessive doors or windows. The bed should be placed against a steady surface and not aligned with the room door.

In terms of career and wealth, it is important to identify and activate positive Facing Stars by aligning with the favourable Chi sector. Health is associated with Sitting Stars, and their negative effects can be weakened by placing a water feature in the corresponding sector. The Tian Yi direction represents the Earth Element and is beneficial for health and career, so tapping into it is advantageous.

Overall, understanding and optimising the flow of Chi through the external and internal factors of a property can enhance its Feng Shui potential and positively impact various aspects of life, such as health, career, and wealth.

UNDERSTANDING THE MOUNTAIN IMPACT AND FENG SHUI

In the realm of Feng Shui, where the term "Feng Shui" translates to "wind and water," the role of mountains becomes significant. While water symbolises the active, Yang aspect of nature, mountains embody the stable, Yin component. In the context of Feng Shui, mountains represent the "mother" and water the "father." The harmonious balance between Yin and Yang is essential for achieving Feng Shui harmony.

MOUNTAINS' ROLE IN FENG SHUI

Understanding that wind carries away Chi (energy) and water accumulates Chi, we must recognise that mountains generate Chi. Mountains, known as the "mothers" of the land, are the source of Chi, which flows down and permeates the environment, animating all life force. Eventually, the Chi settles at the lowest point of the land, where water collects. In this way, water, as the "father," activates the Chi generated by mountains.

Mountains serve multiple functions, akin to nurturing mothers. Not only do they generate Chi, but they also act as protective barriers against wind. By shielding areas from strong winds, mountains create a containment and circulation of Chi within a given space. Consequently, very windy regions often lack mountains.

MOUNTAIN OR WATER: WHICH IS MORE IMPORTANT?

When selecting an ideal Feng Shui area, it is preferable to find both mountains and water. Mountains govern people, including their health, relationships, power, and authority, while water governs wealth. When asked to prioritise between mountains and water, the personal preference leans toward mountains because water can be artificially created, whereas mountains cannot. Moreover, mountains serve as the primary source of Chi, making proximity to the source beneficial. Naturally, an ideal Feng Shui site incorporates both natural mountains and water.

Mountains do not form randomly or by chance; they follow a certain path. Over thousands of years, as the Earth revolves around stars and planets, energy interactions occur. Stars that align with the Earth exert a gravitational pull on its surface, gradually shaping the land. As the Earth's tectonic plates move, the ground rises and settles into forms corresponding to the celestial bodies above.

MOUNTAINS AND YOUR BED

Surprisingly, mountains and beds share similar concepts in Feng Shui. Which is why understanding and looking at your bed placement is such an integral part of your Feng Shui. Mountains represent Yin, just like beds, which serve as the Yin component in internal Feng Shui. Mountains govern health, relationships, power, and so do beds when properly positioned in the right sector. Stability and support are crucial for beds due to their Yin nature, unlike doors, which represent Yang. Therefore, placing beds against glass windows or directly opposite the room door is considered unfavourable.

So what are some common questions and guidelines for your bed or bedroom Feng Shui?

FENG SHUI GUIDELINES FOR BEDS

In terms of internal Feng Shui, beds symbolise external mountain characteristics. So, a well-placed bed not only promotes good health for its occupants but also enhances relationships, social status, respect, and authority.

A Solid Wall Support is an Essential for Bed Placement.

YES, the importance of positioning the head of the bed against a sturdy wall is very important. The reasoning is quite straightforward: a solid wall provides the necessary Yin energy to support the bed, granting it a sense of power and harmony. It forms a harmonious pairing.

Conversely, a bed resting against a window is exposed to excessive Yang energy. This compromises the quality of the bed's energy. Furthermore, in some modern bedrooms, glass panel walls surround the space from all sides, creating an overwhelmingly Yang environment. To counterbalance this, it is advisable to cover any unnecessary glass panels or windows with heavy drapes while sleeping. This helps restore a more Yin-oriented atmosphere to the bedroom.

BED ALIGNMENT

Can you align the head of the bed with a window to face a favourable direction? The answer is it is better not to. It is better to face a negative Life Destiny Palace Gua/Kua direction (see page 102. To work out your favourable and unfavourable directions) that provides a solid wall, ensuring Yin energy supported by Yin.

Example of a crazy common bedroom blunder:

To align the head of the bed with the favourable direction, one might position it at a 45-degree angle in the corner of the room. Not only is this incorrect, it is also highly unfavourable. Consequently, expect restless nights, arguments, ill health, and, in severe cases, even divorce.

Even attempting to cover up the 45-degree angle by constructing a built-in cabinet as a camouflage would not solve the problem.

REGULAR BEDROOM SHAPE IS OPTIMAL.

A square or rectangular bedroom shape is considered the most favourable. Such shapes allow Chi, the vital energy, to flow evenly and steadily as the room serves as a container for it. Conversely, attic rooms with slanted roofs are not ideal for Chi circulation, and rooms with triangular upward roofs lack harmony.

AVOID CEILING BEAMS.

It is widely known to avoid sleeping directly under a ceiling beam. Such irregularities disrupt the Chi flow from above and can direct Chi in an unfavourable manner towards the sleeper. The ideal solution is to create a false ceiling or plaster ceiling to cover the protrusion. If that is not feasible, it is recommended to move the bed away from being directly beneath the beam.

POISON ARROWS IN THE BEDROOM

During the rise in popularity of Feng Shui, the concept of poison arrows became widespread. Suddenly, everyone was talking about being metaphorically 'stabbed in the back' or 'stabbed in the front'. To dispel any confusion about 'poison arrows', it is important to understand that only significant angles can be considered as such. For instance, a corner of a wall (integral to the building's structure) constitutes a genuine poison arrow. On the other hand, those shelves where your books and CDs are placed are unlikely to pose a threat to your well-being.

So, what should you do if you encounter such a situation? Normally, blocking the view (and consequently, the angle itself) with an object like a plant or cabinet would effectively mitigate the impact.

AVOID BED ALIGNMENT WITH YOUR DOOR.

It is advisable to avoid positioning the bed directly in line with the room's door whenever possible.

The rationale behind this guideline is the flow of Chi, which enters the room through the door and directly hits the bed. Since the movement of Chi is considered Yang, it interferes with the Yin nature of the bed.

Occasionally, the bed may be situated in the path of the bathroom door. However, this is not a significant concern. Consider the fact that Chi does not enter from the bathroom or toilet door. Chi only enters through the room door, not the bathroom door.

Therefore, as long as your bathrooms are clean, have a pleasant aroma, and the bathroom door remains closed most of the time, there should be no issue.

BEDROOM WITH A MOUNTAIN VIEW.

Although not a strict rule, bedrooms with an external view of mountains enjoy additional benefits. As mentioned previously, mountains represent the Yin aspect of nature, while beds embody the Yin elements within Feng Shui. When your bedroom overlooks a beautiful, lush mountain, it creates a supportive and positive environment.

WHAT BED MATERIAL YOUR BED IS MADE OFF.

The material used for your bed is not of utmost concern. It could be constructed from metal, wood, plastic, or any other stable material. But by understanding your self-element, bed material can be supportive or unsupportive.

WATERBEDS ARE NOT SUITABLE.

Combining water and mountain elements by using a waterbed is misguided. Beds should be stable like mountains, representing Yin energy. Waterbeds deviate from this principle. Balance is fundamental in Feng Shui, where doors represent Yang and bedrooms represent Yin. Both aspects must harmonise for optimal health and wealth. However, occasional use of a waterbed is acceptable if it is not the primary sleeping bed.

SO, WHAT IS THE DIFFERENCE BETWEEN A MOUNTAIN OR HILL?

Mountains serve as the natural Yin component of the earth's landscape. Are hills considered mountains? Yes, they are. Hills are smaller versions of mountains.

In essence, mountains or hills that emanate positive and harmonious Chi to their surroundings appear lush, green, and healthy. On the other hand, mountains or hills that are rocky, patchy, or fragmented generate aggressive Chi.

Having a view of a good mountain or hill generally contributes to a favourable room environment. Conversely, if your room overlooks an unsightly, rocky mountain, it is not considered ideal.

NATURAL VS MANMADE MOUNTAINS.

Buildings cannot be classified as mountains simply because they do not generate Chi. Buildings lack the Chi generation capacity as they are not naturally born from the interaction between Heaven and Earth over thousands of years.

Nevertheless, for the sake of technical argument, it is possible to "create" a mountain. Firstly, the structure must be at least three stories high or taller. Secondly, it takes time for Chi to be imbued into this "mountain." After all, any substantial physical matter can act as a container for Chi. However, you should expect to wait approximately 10 to 20 years, so an old building may be classed as a mountain.

OVERVIEW OF YOUR BEDROOM.

Take a moment to view your bedroom and the positioning of your bed as the metaphorical "mountain" within your house. Is it stable, protected, and nurturing?

- Do you feel relaxed and safe when entering your bedroom?
- Do you wake up feeling refreshed and ready to conquer the world?
- Do the relationships in your life, especially at home, fill you with hope and gratitude?

If so, these are indications that your bedroom is in a positive sector.

OR

- Do you wake up feeling drained and tired in the morning?
- Do your friends consistently remind you to rest and relax more because you appear constantly tired?
- Are you frequently irritable and inclined to see the negative side of life?
- Is your sex life sluggish, dull, or even non-existent?

These are some signs that your bedroom may be situated in a negative sector or that the internal layout of your bedroom is not ideal. Check if there are an excessive number of glass windows or doors in your room? Too much glass and doors represent Yang energy and may be overshadowing your bedroom yin.

UNDERSTANDING THE WATER IMPACT AND FENG SHUI

Water's role in Feng Shui is crucial and multifaceted. It serves as a gathering point for Chi, accumulating and collecting its energy. Additionally, Water can be used to block, guide, redirect, and retain Chi. As the active component, Water activates and circulates Chi, promoting movement and vitality. However, it's important to note that Water itself does not emit Chi; that role is reserved for Mountains, the Yin component. Wind also plays a significant role in carrying Chi down the Mountains, while Water collects, activates, and propels Chi forward. Ultimately, Water enables the usability and activation of Chi in an area, and it can be strategically utilised to control Chi flow and concentrate it in specific locations. Without Water, even an area with favourable landforms and Chi potential remains untapped.

"In classical Feng Shui, Water is regarded as the foremost representation of the Yang element."

Water plays a vital role as an activator in Feng Shui. It can positively impact various aspects, including wealth, health improvement, relationship enhancement, conflict resolution, fertility support, and overall household harmony. However, the specific outcomes it activates depend on the existing Chi, such as the Flying Star, in the surrounding area. It is incorrect to assume that Water Feng Shui solely guarantees wealth or financial success. Instead, Water Feng Shui can also contribute to good health, harmonious relationships, and finding love.

In Feng Shui, Water has two distinct qualities. Slow and meandering water, known as "sentimental" water, is preferred in Feng Shui. On the other hand, fast-flowing and turbulent water is considered unfavourable. Water can reflect Chi, create barriers for Chi collection, and redirect Chi, but this applies to both positive and negative Chi.

Natural water formations like lakes, creeks, and rivers are highly valued in Feng Shui compared to man-made water creations such as fountains or swimming pools. Natural water formations have the advantage of scale and being harmoniously aligned with their surroundings. They allow Chi to flow naturally, making it more abundant and potent. In contrast, man-made environments require more effort to manipulate Chi and direct it to desired areas. While water can be artificially created, replicating the power of natural mountain formations is nearly impossible.

FENG SHUI BASICS
THE FIVE ELEMENTS

The Five Elements play a significant role in Feng Shui, Four Pillars of Destiny, and Chinese Metaphysics. They symbolise Chi and should not be interpreted literally. In the analysis of Four Pillars of Destiny and Bazi, these elements represent important characteristics within a person's chart.

FIVE TYPES OF CHI

Element	Representation	Properties	Shapes	Colors
Earth	Trustworthiness, stability, wealth	Attractive, dense, stable	Square	Yellow, Orange, Brown
Metal	Justice, authority, altruism	Sharp, pointing, piercing	Round	White, gold, silver
Water	Wisdom, thoughts, intelligence	Runs downhill, free/unbound	Wavy	Blue, black
Wood	Life, growth, benevolence, education	Grows outwards, enduring	Oblong	Green
Fire	Beauty, elegance, passion	Spreads in every direction, radiates heat	Sharp	Red, Purple, Pink

HE TU

The Five Elements in the He Tu It is important to remember that the He Tu and Luo Shu are distinct from the Eight Trigrams (Ba gua). The He Tu represents the theoretical model of perfect universal forces, where there is no movement, evolution, or concept of time.

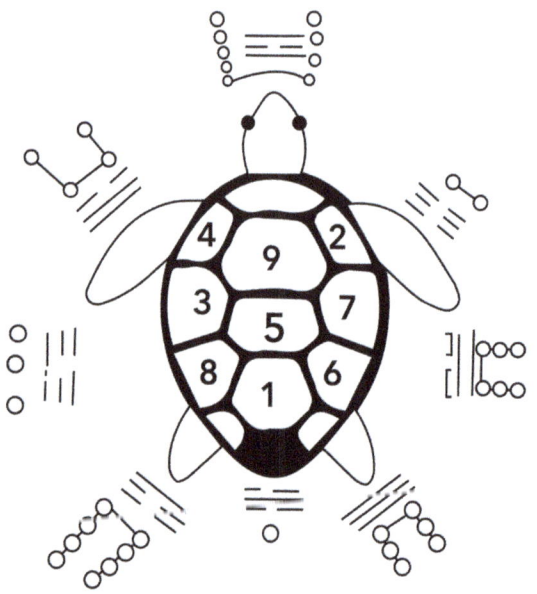

LUO SHU

On the other hand, the Luo Shu represents the cyclical nature of the universe, encompassing birth, growth, sickness, extinction, and other aspects that signify movement and evolution. The Luo Shu serves as the foundation for Feng Shui applications such as Flying Stars Ba qua and Eight Mansions, as it reflects the actual compass directions within a building. Additionally, the Luo Shu contains the elemental locations for the Five Elements.

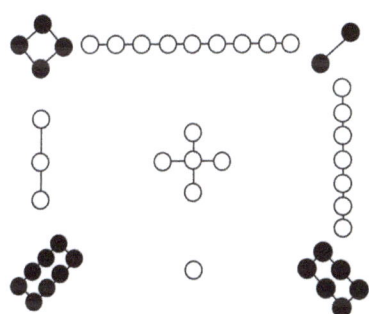

4	9	2
3	5	7
8	1	6

You may not yet know your House's Chi map or Flying Stars. But with a comprehensive understanding of Flying Stars, one can predict future events affecting the occupants.

It's important to note that while Flying Stars produces quick and dynamic effects, these effects are relatively short-term and not as influential as (Landform) Feng

Shui. Flying Stars is a goal-oriented system that can reveal hidden information about a property's occupants, including aspects like character, health, wealth, and relationships. (Refer to page 190 for flying star meanings)

Another rule about Chi In the study of the Bagua, Eight Mansions and Flying Stars, it is not necessary to divide all nine grids/sectors meticulously and precisely into equal sizes. Chi, as a form of energy, expands and contracts like matter and energy in physics. It can be transferred from one form to another. Therefore, it suffices to approximate the size or area of each sector/grid for analysis purposes.

MOUNTAINS

THE ACTIVATORS/ENHANCERS OF SITTING STARS

While Water activates/enhances Facing Stars, Mountains activate/enhance Sitting Stars. The type and elemental form of the mountains present determine the type of Chi influencing the Sitting Star. This emphasizes the significance of external Forms in determining the internal Feng Shui of a property.

FLYING STARS IN MOTION: MAKING WHAT'S GOOD, BETTER!

To optimise the Feng Shui of a property, it is crucial to identify the prominent Facing and Sitting Stars. This knowledge helps determine the ideal locations for the main door, bedrooms, and kitchen. For example, in Period 9, the prominent stars are number 9, number 1, and number 2.

The first step in learning how to fly the stars is to become familiar with the Luo Shu. It represents the sequence or order of movements in a Flying Stars chart, depicting the pattern of Chi's movement. This pattern remains constant and is applied to any star chart, including Natal, annual, or yearly charts. As this book is not about teaching you to fly the stars, flying star charts are provided on pages 137-145.

FLYING STARS & THE TIMELINESS OF STARS

Each Flying Star in the system represents a different type of Chi. Since Chi is dynamic and constantly changing, every Star has its own cycle of strength, reflecting the different stages or phases of the represented Chi. In the Nine Palaces Grid method of Flying Stars, each Star is assigned a number from number 1 to number 9. Therefore, each number in a Flying Stars Chart represents a particular Star. The concept of the "Timeliness" of Stars refers to the positive and negative effects of these Stars in conjunction with the passage of Time. For instance, in Period 9 (2024-2043), the most prosperous Star is number 9.

SO, WHAT IS ALL THIS TALK ABOUT FLYING STARS?

Flying Stars, also known as Xuan Kong Fei Xing or Nine Stars, is a classical Feng Shui system that assigns specific energies or influences to different directions and sectors within a space. It is based on the belief that energy, or Chi, is not stagnant and changes over time.

In Flying Stars Feng Shui, there are nine stars or energies represented by numbers from 1 to 9. These stars are associated with different elements, such as Wood, Fire, Earth, Metal, and Water, and each star carries a particular quality or influence.

The Flying Stars are determined by a combination of factors, including the Period in which a building was constructed and its facing direction. These factors are used to calculate a natal chart, also known as a Flying Stars chart, which reveals the distribution of the stars in the various sectors of the building.

Each year, month, and day, the Flying Stars shift their positions within the chart, creating different energy combinations in different sectors. These energy combinations can have positive or negative effects on the occupants of the space.

Feng Shui practitioners use the Flying Stars system to analyse and enhance the energy of space. They may recommend specific adjustments, such as the placement of remedies or enhancements, to harmonise and optimise the energy in each sector. These adjustments can be made by activating favourable stars or suppressing unfavourable ones using colors, objects, symbols, and other Feng Shui cures.

By understanding the Flying Stars and their movements, practitioners aim to create a balanced and harmonious environment that supports the well-being, success, and prosperity of the occupants. It is believed that working with the Flying Stars can help harness auspicious energies and minimise the impact of inauspicious ones.

Flying Stars allow, advise and help you understand balance for each area of your home to bring good energy for occupants and to be able to dissipate any bad energy.

The Flying Stars system in Feng Shui focuses on the short-term energy influences within a space. It considers the positive and negative stars that appear during specific Periods. Understanding these stars and their attributes allows us to enhance beneficial energies and mitigate unfavourable ones.

In Flying Stars Feng Shui, each sector of a home is assigned a Star represented by a Number. Understanding the positive and negative attributes of each of the Nine Stars is essential. However, it is important to remember that this is a generalised perspective, and some Stars can be inherently positive or negative depending on various circumstances.

Two significant factors that influence the Stars are timeliness and forms. A Star appearing at the right or prosperous timing carries positive Chi and strengthens its influence. Conversely, negative forms could amplify the negative aspects of a Star, especially if the Chi produced or conducted by these forms directly affects the property. Negative forms can compound the ill-effects of negative Stars, and vice versa.

While each Star is identified by a number and colour, it is important not to infer too much about a Star solely based on these characteristics. The numbers and colours are primarily used for easier identification, as stipulated in the ancient classical texts.

Flying Stars are applied to the Natal Chart of a property, and Annual and Monthly Flying Stars Charts are used to determine the positive energies for the year and different months, respectively.

PERIOD 9
THE GRAND RESET

To explore additional aspects related to Period 9 fulfillment and its potential impact on our lives, let us examine the implications and components of Period 9, along with the opportunities for external application and personalisation. Can we alter our destiny? Our lives and the outcomes we experience are closely intertwined with the choices we make or refrain from making. We possess the power to change our course and reshape our future trajectory.

THE COSMIC TRINITY UNVEILED

In Period 9, a unique opportunity arises, allowing us to mould our destiny by blending personal potential with environmental influences. The year 2023 has been marked by chaos and instability, serving as a transformative phase leading up to the arrival of Period 9 on February 4th, 2024, and extending until 2043. Feng Shui, firmly rooted in mathematical principles, provides a framework to grasp and harness the influence emanating from the Solar System.

THE CELESTIAL DANCE OF PLANETS

Let us now explore the significance of Period 9. "Li" Gua, the star associated with this period, represents the expansion of the mind and the unveiling of intangible forces. Period 9 embodies hope, spirituality, miracles, and abundance, presenting a realm brimming with possibilities.

UNVEILING THE POWER OF NUMBER 9

The number 9 derives from the "Li" Gua trigram. In the realm of the Five Elements, Fire stands as the sole transformative force capable of instigating change. It possesses the power to consume Wood, melt Metal, and influence the interactions between Earth and Water. Fire holds a unique ability to transform and impact all other elements within its domain. Hence, Period 9 symbolises the phase of the "Middle-Aged Woman," which, considering modern practices and the ability of women to maintain a youthful appearance, encompasses a broader demographic.

EMBRACING THE ESSENCE OF PERIOD 9

In order to fully embrace the essence of Period 9, it is important to understand key components that hold significance and are reflected in this period. These components include:

Middle-aged women are women aged between 40 and 60 who can maintain a youthful appearance through modern practices.

The term "middle daughter" refers to individuals who hold the position of being the middle daughter within their family structure.

Plus-size women are individuals with a fuller figure or a tendency towards weight gain, reflecting the ongoing trend of increasing body sizes.

Superficiality focuses on individuals who prioritise outer beauty without emphasising inner depth or substance.

In the context of Feng Shui, the south direction is associated with the component of the south direction.

The phoenix, symbolising new birth, represents rejuvenation and new beginnings.

Expressing authenticity encourages individuals to showcase their best qualities and genuine selves to the world.

Luxurious possessions encompass opulent belongings such as high-end properties, cars, and jewellery.

"Niche is the new rich" emphasises the idea that targeting a specific and specialised market can lead to wealth and success.

Niche markets are specialised areas of focus, such as luxury goods, technology, and religion.

Heightened spirituality refers to the increasing number of individuals who are seeking spiritual growth and understanding.

Manifestation involves the process of transforming desires and aspirations into tangible reality.

By understanding and embracing these key components, individuals can align themselves with the essence of Period 9 and harness its potential.

UNVEILING THE DAWN OF PERIOD 9

There exist two perspectives regarding the onset of the 1st wave of Period 9 and its associated trends:

EARLY HEAVEN PERIOD 9 (2017-2024):

Many hold the belief that the first wave of Period 9 commenced in 2017, marked by significant developments in the construction industry, the rise of online shopping, and the emergence of small businesses. Notable success stories include the growth of ventures like Bumble (launched in 2014), Zero (launched in 2006), After Pay (launched in 2013), Zoom (launched in 2011), and Canva (launched in 2012). This period also witnessed the emergence of risks associated with bitcoin and NFT crypto investments. Furthermore, 2017 witnessed a notable rise in the emergence and growth of female leaders across various fields, exemplified by figures like Kamala Harris, Jacinda Ardern, Whitney Wolfe (Bumble Founder), and Melanie Perkins (Canva Co-Founder), among others.

LATER HEAVEN PERIOD 9 (2024-2043):

The second wave, known as Later Heaven, is set to commence in 2024 with the infusion of Yin Fire energy. Yin Fire is akin to a flickering and elusive candle flame. Fire symbolizes various qualities such as speed, vision, emotions, inspiration, and constant change. This dynamic element is associated with the rise of addictive behaviours like excessive social media use and gaming. Fire represents the pursuit of experiences and the desire to look and feel good. Consequently, an increase in concerts and immersive experiences is anticipated. Fire also embodies spirituality and ceaseless energy, disrupting the traditional 9-5 job structure. However, the lack of substance in Yin Fire may lead to a surge in fake news and scam alerts. In this context, the Li Gua represents beauty, indicating that visually appealing products and offerings will gain prominence in the market.

A DISCOURSE OF TRANSITION

Some practitioners hold the belief that Period 9 in Feng Shui began in 2020, suggesting an earlier transition than traditionally acknowledged. They support this viewpoint by pointing to significant global events and shifts that occurred around that time, such as the COVID-19 pandemic and its profound impact on society. These events exemplify the transformative energy associated with a new period. Additionally, advancements in technology, the rise of digital platforms, and the increased focus on sustainability and environmental awareness are seen as indicators of Period 9's influence. While this perspective is not universally accepted, it highlights the ongoing discourse and interpretation surrounding the onset of Period 9 and its effects on our lives and surroundings.

THE LEGACY OF PERIOD 9: LASTING IMPACT

WORLD EVENTS, TRENDS, AND HEALTH ISSUES (1843-1863)

The 19th century witnessed an array of significant world events, cultural shifts, and health challenges that left an indelible mark on history. Exploring these events and trends offers valuable insights into the social, political, and medical landscapes of that era.

POLITICAL AND SOCIAL TRANSFORMATIONS:

Revolutions of 1848: The year 1848 heralded a wave of revolutions across Europe, driven by demands for political freedoms and socioeconomic reforms. Uprisings erupted in countries like France, Germany, Italy, and Hungary, resulted in the overthrow of monarchies and the establishment of constitutional regimes.

American Civil War: The Civil War (1861-1865) stands as one of the most consequential events in American history, dividing the nation along ideological lines and sparking a bloody conflict between the Northern Union and the Southern Confederacy. The war had far-reaching consequences, ultimately leading to the abolition of slavery in the United States.

Industrial Revolution: The mid-19th century marked the apex of the Industrial Revolution, witnessing rapid technological advancements that transformed manufacturing processes and transportation systems. Factories proliferated, railways expanded, and a myriad of inventions reshaped society, leading to urbanisation.

SCIENTIFIC ADVANCEMENTS:

Charles Darwin and Evolution: In 1859, Charles Darwin published his seminal work, "On the Origin of Species," introducing the theory of evolution. Darwin's groundbreaking ideas challenged traditional religious beliefs and profoundly impacted fields such as biology, anthropology, and our understanding of human origins.

Germ Theory and Medical Progress: The 19th century witnessed remarkable strides in medical knowledge and practice. In the 1840s, Ignaz Semmelweis championed the significance of hand hygiene in reducing childbed fever. Additionally, the germ theory of disease, pioneered by Louis Pasteur and others, paved the way for understanding infectious diseases and the development of preventive measures.

HEALTH CHALLENGES:

Cholera Epidemics: The mid-19th century witnessed devastating cholera outbreaks across the globe, particularly in urban areas with inadequate sanitation. These epidemics caused widespread fatalities and led to the implementation of public health measures such as improved sewage systems and the establishment of health boards.

Mental Health Awareness: The 19th century witnessed a growing recognition of mental health issues. Pioneers like Dorothea Dix advocated for improved treatment of the mentally ill, leading to the establishment of asylums and reforms in mental healthcare.

Medical Advancements and Anaesthesia: The period between 1843 and 1863 witnessed remarkable developments in the field of surgery. The use of anaesthesia, pioneered by William Morton and others, revolutionised surgical procedures, reducing pain and increasing patient survival rates.

In conclusion, the years between 1843 and 1863 were a transformative period in world history, characterised by political upheavals, scientific breakthroughs, and health challenges. The revolutions of 1848 and the American Civil War reshaped political landscapes, while advancements in science and medicine, such as Darwin's theory of Evolution and the germ theory of disease, revolutionised our understanding of the natural world and human health. The health issues of the time, including cholera epidemics and mental health awareness, prompted significant reforms in public health and medical practices. By exploring this pivotal period, we gain a deeper appreciation for the factors that have shaped the world as we know it today.

FENG SHUI AND THE ELEMENTS: UNDERSTANDING PERIOD 9

In the study of Feng Shui, a unique approach is employed to interpret solar system energy by associating it with stars and using numerical designations instead of planet names.

PLANETARY INFLUENCES AND ELEMENTAL ASSOCIATIONS

Each planet in the realm of planetary influences has its own elemental association. For example, Mercury is linked to water, Venus aligns with metal, Earth represents itself, Mars embodies fire, Jupiter corresponds to wood, and Saturn aligns with earth. Jupiter holds great significance and is considered the most important planet in metaphysical studies. In Period 9, the conjunction of Jupiter and Saturn, known as the "great conjunction," occurs every 20 years and marks a significant shift leading to the start of a new period. As we approach 2040, the transitional energies of Period 1 will gradually become perceptible. Jupiter's influence brings a sense of adventure and expansion, while Saturn adds its unique qualities to the celestial tapestry.

THE IMPORTANCE OF BALANCE AND LIFE FORCE EXPANSION

Success in Feng Shui is closely tied to balance, and the system emphasises the recognition of Life Force expansion (Bazi). Feng Shui explores the concept of environmental life force, highlighting the ability to tap into and harmonise with one's surroundings. By positioning oneself optimally within the environment, life force can be enhanced. Traditional Feng Shui focuses on correct positioning rather than activation, although achieving ideal positioning can be challenging when working with existing homes and environments.

UNDERSTANDING THE FIVE ELEMENTS IN FENG SHUI

The Five Elements play a significant role in Feng Shui, Four Pillars of Destiny, and Chinese Metaphysics. They symbolise Chi and should not be interpreted literally. In a Four Pillars of Destiny and Bazi analysis, these elements represent important characteristics within a person's chart. The Five Elements are Earth, Metal, Water, Wood, and Fire, each having unique properties, shapes, and colours.

DIFFERENTIATING HE TU AND LUO SHU

It is essential to differentiate between the He Tu and Luo Shu concepts in Feng Shui. The He Tu represents the theoretical model of perfect universal forces, devoid of movement, evolution, or the concept of time. On the other hand, the Luo Shu represents the cyclical nature of the universe, encompassing birth, growth, sickness, extinction, and other aspects that signify movement and evolution. The Luo Shu serves as the foundation for Feng Shui applications such as Flying Stars Ba gua and Eight Mansions, reflecting actual compass directions within a building and providing elemental locations for the Five Elements.

OPTIMISING YOUR LIVING SPACE FOR PERIOD 9 FULFILLMENT

When it comes to the growth and fulfillment of your life, understanding your environment and its impact on you is crucial. By assessing your environment, you can determine the need for leveraging Feng Shui to align your environment with your personal energy. Through strategic positioning and activation of sectors, you can create a potent synergy that amplifies positive outcomes.

OPTIMISING YOUR LIVING SPACE

While changing your physical residence may not always be possible, there are alternative approaches to optimise your living space. By strategically utilising positions and sectors, you can activate and enhance the energy within your home. It's important to recognise that every country and dwelling has favourable and unfavourable Feng Shui areas. Focus on harnessing the potential of the most advantageous areas available to you.

BUYING AND FULFILLMENT FOR PERIOD 9

To ensure Period 9 fulfillment in Feng Shui, consider external aspects when selecting a house or building. Seek properties with favourable building life force energy, known as "good Feng Shui." Factors such as location, orientation, and overall energy flow of the structure are crucial. By prioritising these external elements, you can align your living or working spaces with the positive energy of Period 9 and enhance the overall Feng Shui of your environment.

QUALIFYING THE BEST AREAS

To identify healthy land and environment, consider two indicators: balanced Yin and Yang energies. Mountains represent Yin, signifying fulfillment and well-being, while water represents Yang, symbolising achievement and wealth. Seek areas with natural forms of mountains and water to harness their positive effects on happiness, health, wealth, and success.

CHOOSING BETWEEN MOUNTAINS AND WATER

Ideally, it is beneficial to have both mountains and water features in your living space. However, if you can only choose one, consider your personal priorities. A mountain feature brings long-term happiness and people luck, while a water feature is more important for business and wealth luck. Select based on what matters most to you.

POSITIONING YOUR BUILDING

Consider the direction your building faces, as it plays a significant role in Feng Shui. Analyse directional aspects and apply Feng Shui principles to optimise the energetic flow and enhance positive qualities of the space. Utilise the Luo Shu and He Tu theories to guide your decisions.

BALANCING YIN AND YANG ENERGIES

Maintaining a balance between Yin and Yang forces is essential in Feng Shui. In Period 9, Yin and Yang energies depend on the facing direction of your property. If facing Yin, observe the presence of Yang elements such as water, and if facing Yang, ensure the presence of Yin elements such as mountains for equilibrium.

CHOOSING THE RIGHT ELEMENTS

The specific facing direction of your property is not the primary consideration. Focus on fulfillment with Feng Shui principles and assess whether you need the presence of mountains and/or water based on your direction. Closer views of mountains enhance the well-being and luck of your family, while a water view benefits business, career, and financial luck.

CRUCIAL SECTORS FOR PERIOD 9

During Period 9, the "South" sector holds immense importance and should be present in your home or building. This sector represents the timeliest star and possesses significant power during this period.

Ensuring Your Lifestyle Sector is not missing.

Your "Lifestyle" sector, also referred to as your life star, magic number, Gua, or Kua, should never be absent from your home or apartment. Its presence is vital as it signifies the supporting energy necessary for your well-being.

The significance of your Chinese Zodiac Sign is on par with your "life star." For instance, if your Chinese zodiac sign is the "OX," it is associated with the Northeast direction. Therefore, it is crucial to ensure that the Northeast sector is present and not missing in your living or working space.

Each Chinese zodiac sign corresponds to a specific direction, and it is essential to have the corresponding sector in your living or working space. Here are the zodiac signs and their respective directions that must not be missing:

Rat: North

Ox: Northeast

Tiger: Northeast

Rabbit: East

Dragon: Southeast

Snake: Southeast

Horse: South

Goat: Southwest

Monkey: Southwest

Rooster: West

Dog: Northwest

Pig: Northwest

To create a Period 9 compatible living or working space that supports your well-being and success, it is essential to maximise the utilisation of the central area. Avoid leaving it empty or unused and instead fill it with appropriate furniture, decor, or functional elements. The centre holds great importance in Feng Shui, and its proper activation contributes to the overall balance and harmony of the space.

To ensure your property meets Period 9 principles and provides optimal support, follow this quick checklist:

REFRESH - QUICK PROPERTY CHECKLIST

Look for either a mountain or water view:

Mountain signifies good luck for people and relationships.

Water signifies prosperity and abundance.

Verify that the "South" sector of the property is present and usable. This sector holds significant power in Period 9 as per example page 97 highlighted.

Check that your life star is not located in a missing sector.

Ensure that your Chinese zodiac animal sector is not missing.

By addressing these key points, you can assess the compatibility of your home with Period 9 principles and determine its potential to create a supportive environment for your well-being and success. Keep in mind that having a square or rectangular house is ideal as it minimises the chances of missing sectors and enhances overall harmony.

This simple checklist serves as a helpful guide to evaluate your home's compatibility and its ability to create a supportive environment for your well-being and success.

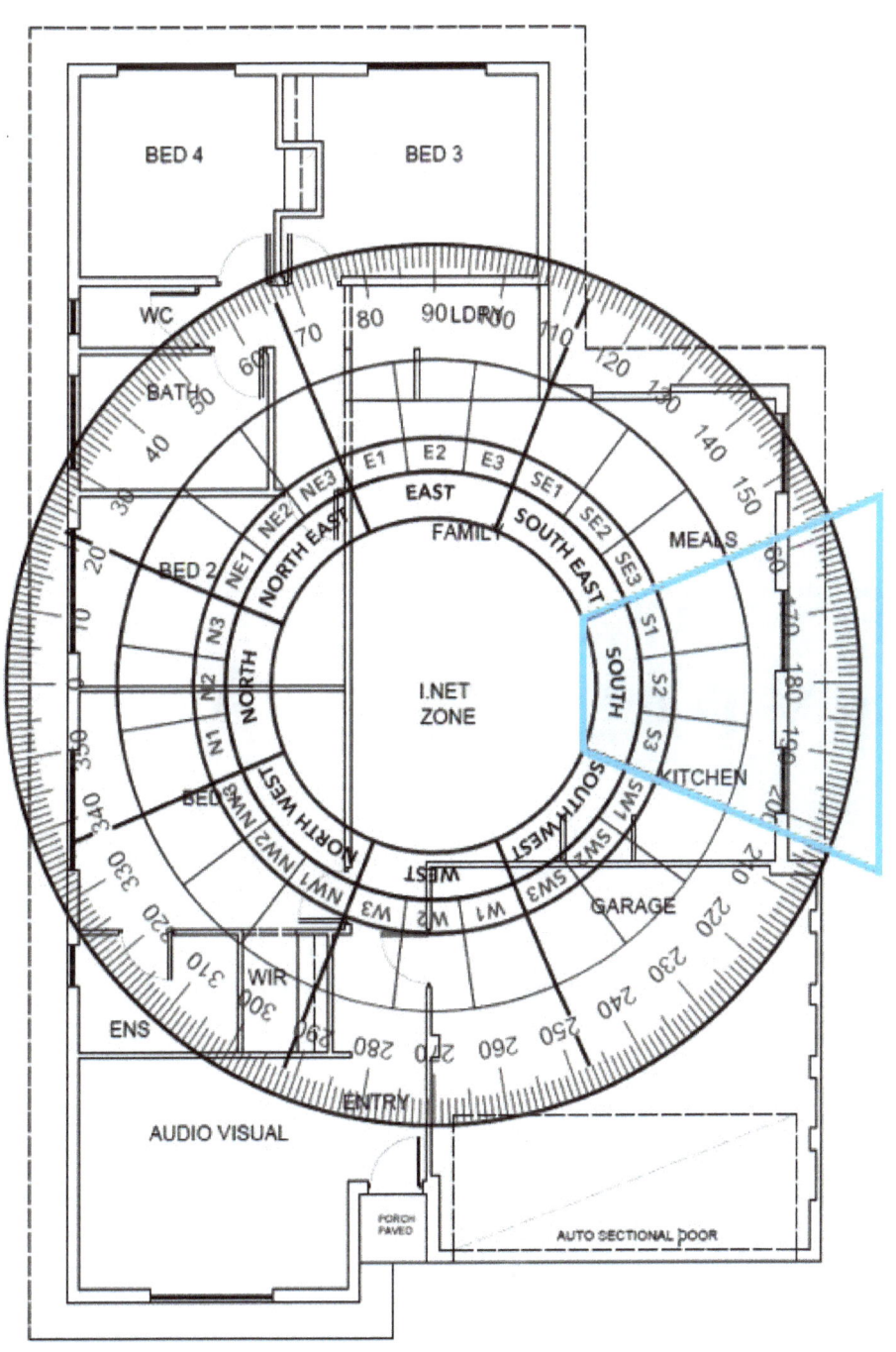

UNDERSTANDING LIFE DESTINY PALACE GUA OR KUA

Understanding your Life Destiny Palace Gua or Kua Directions, comes from the Feng Shui formula of Eight Mansions, School of Feng Shui and is one of the easier and more popular methods used to determine the favourable and unfavourable location of a house. Its method analyses whether you are compatible with the house and finds out your favourable and unfavourable personal directions that promote productivity at work and in relationships, and good health, wealth, and successful academic pursuits.

In this formula of Feng Shui, a building or house is divided into nine palaces (sectors), one being in the center and eight of which correspond to the eight magnetic directions. These palaces are North, South, East, West (cardinal directions), Northeast, Southeast, Southwest, and Northwest (inter-cardinal directions).

Each of the eight magnetic directions holds a different kind of Chi which will influence the respective palace and the person living in it, either favourable or unfavourable. In other words, the energies of the Chi from a given direction can be in harmony or out of harmony for yourself and energy.

This formula is quite easy to learn and apply; it is not as complicated as some of the other Schools. It is, however, a stagnant school of Feng Shui, but it is one that you can use anywhere you go. You can use it when you are buying a block of land, going for an interview, applying for a loan, positioning your bed, or even going to a function.

Let's look at the formula to work out your own personal Kua number from which you will determine your four favourable or auspicious directions and locations, and your four unfavourable or inauspicious directions and locations; what they mean, and how to use them.

THE FORMULA

How to calculate your Life Palace Destiny Number often referred to as Gua or Kua.

Or refer to page 102 for quick reference.

For FEMALES

- Add the last two digits of your year of birth together.
- If you get two digits, add them again until you get only one number, then add 5.
- Number 5 is a special number, as there is no Gua 5.
- Females replace number 5 by number 8 to get Gua 8.

For MALES

- Add the last two digits of your year of birth together.
- If you get two digits, add them again until you get only one number, then deduct from 10.
- Number 5 is a special number, as there is no Gua 5.
- Males replace number 2 by number 2 to get Gua 2.

For example, if you were born 1994, you add the nine and the four together.

Example: 9 + 4 = 13
Then add the one and three to get a single digit number.

Example: 1 + 3 = 4
For a female, add five to the final number. The answer is the person's Life Palace Destiny number.

Example: 4 + 5 = 9. The Life Palace Destiny number is nine (9) for this person.
For a male, subtract ten from the final figure. The answer is the person's Kua number.

Example: 4 - 10 = -6. The Life Palace Destiny number is six (6) for this person.
There are, however, some variables to consider:

Born in January: If you were born in January, then you need to take the year before as per the Lunar Calendar and not the Western Calendar; the transition date for the year is the 4th of February. Therefore, if you were born on the 4th of January 1975, you would take 1974 and add the seven and the four together.

Example: 7 + 4 = 11
        1 + 1 = 2

Complete the formula adding five if you are a female or subtracting ten if you are male.

Year 2000 and beyond: For those born in or after 2000, you need to do the following:

Male: Take away nine instead of ten from the final number.

Example: 2001 would be 1 - 9 = -8, so the Kua number would be eight (8).

Female: Add six instead of five to the final number.

Example: 2001 would be 1 + 6 = 7, so the Kua number would be seven (7).

The number five: If you come up with a five as the final number, it will need to be changed as there is no five in many Schools of Feng Shui due to it being considered negative. Therefore, a female it gets changed to a number eight (8), and a male it gets changed to the number two (2).

Example For FEMALES

1991
9 + 1 = 10
10 = 1
1 + 5 = 6

Life Destiny or Palace Number is 6

DIRECTIONS EAST AND WEST

Directions are also broken up into two groups, either East or West. East number people belong to numbers one, (1), three (3), four (4) or nine (9). West number people belong to numbers two (2), six (6) seven (7) and eight (8).

Gua Directions is very popular, and its great merit lies in its easy practicality, which anyone can benefit from. Once you know you are in the most favourable direction, it is then only a matter of taking some time to check the directions you're sitting and facing when you sleep, sit, work or study.

YOUR LIFE DESTINY PALACE GUA/KUA NUMBERS

Look up your Gua number according to your birthdate, then check for your auspicious and inauspicious directions.

YEAR OF BIRTH	ANIMAL SIGN	HEAVENLY STEM	BORN BETWEEN…	MALE	FEMALE
1900	Rat	Metal	Jan 31, 1900-Feb 18, 1901	1	5
1901	Ox	Metal	Feb 19,1901 - Feb 7, 1902	9	6
1902	Tiger	Water	Feb 8, 1902-Jan 28, 1903	8	7
1903	Rabbit	Water	Jan 29,1903-Feb 28, 1904	7	8
1904	Dragon	Wood	Feb 16,1904- Feb 3,1905	6	9
1905	Snake	Wood	Feb 4, 1905-Jan 24, 1906	5	1
1906	Horse	Fire	Jan 25,1906-Feb 12,1907	4	2
1907	Goat	Fire	Feb 13, 1907- Feb 1, 1908	3	3
1908	Monkey	Earth	Feb 2,1908-Jan 21, 1909	2	4
1909	Rooster	Earth	Jan 22,1909- Feb 9,1910	1	5
1910	Dog	Metal	Feb 10, 1910-Jan 29,1911	9	6
1911	Pig	Metal	Jan 30,1911 - Feb 17,1912	8	7
1912	Rat	Water	Feb 18, 1912-Feb 5, 1913	7	8
1913	Ox	Water	Feb 6, 1913-Jan 25, 1914	6	9
1914	Tiger	Wood	Jan 26,1914- Feb 13, 1915	5	1

1915	Rabbit	Wood	Feb 14,1915-Feb 2,1916	4	2
1916	Dragon	Fire	Feb 3,1916-Jan 22,1917	3	3
1917	Snake	Fire	Jan 23, 1917- Feb 10, 1918	2	4
1918	Horse	Earth	Feb 11,1918-Jan 31, 1919	1	5
1919	Goat	Earth	Feb 1,1919-Feb 19, 1920	9	6
1920	Monkey	Metal	Feb 20, 1920-Feb 7, 1921	8	7
1921	Rooster	Metal	Feb 8,1921 - Jan 27, 1922	7	8
1922	Dog	Water	Jan 28, 1922-Feb 15, 1923	6	9
1923	Pig	Water	Feb 16,1923- Feb 4, 1924	5	1
1924	Rat	Wood	Feb 5, 1924-Jan 23, 1925	4	2
1925	Ox	Wood	Jan 24, 1925- Feb 12, 1926	3	3
1926	Tiger	Fire	Feb 13,1926- Feb 1,1927	2	4
1927	Rabbit	Fire	Feb 2, 1927-Jan 22, 1928	1	5
1928	Dragon	Earth	Jan 23,1928- Feb 9, 1929	9	6
1929	Snake	Earth	Feb 10,1929 - Jan 29,1930	8	7
1930	Horse	Metal	Jan 30,1930- Feb 16 1931	7	8
1931	Goat	Metal	Feb 17,1931 - Feb 5, 1932	6	9
1932	Monkey	Water	Feb 6, 1932-Jan 25,1933	5	1
1933	Rooster	Water	Jan 26, 1933-Feb 13, 1934	4	2
1934	Dog	Wood	Feb 14,1934- Feb 3,1935	3	3
1935	Pig	Wood	Feb 4, 1935-Jan 23, 1936	2	4
1936	Rat	Fire	Jan 24, 1936- Feb 10,1937	1	5
1937	Ox	Fire	Feb 11,1937-Jan 30,1938	9	6
1938	Tiger	Earth	Jan 31,1938-Feb 18, 1939	8	7
1939	Rabbit	Earth	Feb 19, 1939- Feb 7, 1940	7	8
1940	Dragon	Metal	Feb 8, 1940-Jan 26, 1941	6	9

1941	Snake	Metal	Jan 27, 1941 - Feb 14, 1942	5	1
1942	Horse	Water	Feb 15, 1942 - Feb 4,1943	4	2
1943	Goat	Water	Feb 5, 1943-Jan 24, 1944	3	3
1944	Monkey	Wood	Jan 25,1944-Feb 12,1945	2	4
1945	Rooster	Wood	Feb 13, 1945 - Feb 1, 1946	1	5
1946	Dog	Fire	Feb 2, 1946-Jan 21, 1947	9	6
1947	Pig	Fire	Jan 22, 1947-Feb 9, 1948	8	7
1948	Rat	Earth	Feb 10, 1948-Jan 28, 1949	7	8
1949	Ox	Earth	Jan 29, 1949-Feb 16, 1950	6	9
1950	Tiger	Metal	Feb 17, 1950- Feb 5,1951	5	1
1951	Rabbit	Metal	Feb 6, 1951 - Jan 26 1952	4	2
1952	Dragon	Water	Jan 27,1952 - Feb 13,1953	3	3
1953	Snake	Water	Feb 14, 1953- Feb 2, 1954	2	4
1954	Horse	Wood	Feb 3, 1954-Jan 23, 1955	1	5
1955	Goat	Wood	Jan 24, 1955-Feb 11, 1956	9	6
1956	Monkey	Fire	Feb 12,1956-Jan 30, 1957	8	7
1957	Rooster	Fire	Jan 31, 1957-Feb 17, 1958	7	8
1958	Dog	Earth	Feb 18, 1958-Feb 7 1959	6	9
1959	Pig	Earth	Feb 8, 1959-Jan 27, 1960	5	1
1960	Rat	Metal	Jan 28, 1960 - Feb 14, 1961	4	2
1961	Ox	Metal	Feb 15, 1961 - Feb 4, 1962	3	3
1962	Tiger	Water	Feb 5, 1962 - Jan 24, 1963	2	4
1963	Rabbit	Water	Jan 25, 1963- Feb 12 1964	1	5
1964	Dragon	Wood	Feb 13, 1964-Feb 1,1965	9	6
1965	Snake	Wood	Feb 2, 1965-Jan 20, 1966	8	7

1966	Horse	Fire	Jan 21,1966-Feb 8,1967	7	8
1967	Goat	Fire	Feb 9,1967-Jan 29,1968	6	9
1968	Monkey	Earth	Jan 30, 1968-Feb 16, 1969	5	1
1969	Rooster	Earth	Feb 17, 1969-Feb 5, 1970	4	2
1970	Dog	Metal	Feb 6, 1970-Jan 26,1971	3	3
1971	Pig	Metal	Jan 27, 1971 - Feb 14, 1972	2	4
1972	Rat	Water	Feb 15, 1972-Feb 2, 1973	1	5
1973	Ox	Water	Feb 3, 1973-Jan 22, 1974	9	6
1974	Tiger	Wood	Jan 23, 1974-Feb 10, 1975	8	7
1975	Rabbit	Wood	Feb 11, 1975 - Jan 30, 1976	7	8
1976	Dragon	Fire	Jan 31, 1976-Feb 17 1977	6	9
1977	Snake	Fire	Feb 18,1977- Feb 6, 1978	5	1
1978	Horse	Earth	Feb 7, 1978 - Jan 27, 1979	4	2
1979	Goat	Earth	Jan 28, 1979 - Feb 15, 1980	3	3
1980	Monkey	Metal	Feb 16, 1980- Feb 4, 1981	2	4
1981	Rooster	Metal	Feb 5, 1981 - Jan 24, 1982	1	5
1982	Dog	Water	Jan 25, 1982-Feb12, 1983	9	6
1983	Pig	Water	Feb 13,1983- Feb 1,1984	8	7
1984	Rat	Wood	Feb 2,1984- Feb 19, 1985	7	8
1985	Ox	Wood	Feb 20, 1985-Feb 8, 1986	6	9
1986	Tiger	Fire	Feb 9, 1986-Jan 28, 1987	5	1
1987	Rabbit	Fire	Jan 29, 1987- Feb 16, 1988	4	2
1988	Dragon	Earth	Feb 17, 1988- Feb 5, 1989	3	3
1989	Snake	Earth	Feb 6, 1989 Jan 26, 1990	2	4
1990	Horse	Metal	Jan 27,1990 - Feb 14,1991	1	5

1991	Goat	Metal	Feb 15, 1991 - Feb 3, 1992	9	6
1992	Monkey	Water	Feb 4, 1992-Jan 22, 1993	8	7
1993	Rooster	Water	Jan 23,1993 - Feb 9, 1994	7	8
1994	Dog	Wood	Feb 10, 1994-Jan 30, 1995	6	9
1995	Pig	Wood	Jan 31, 1995-Feb 18, 1996	5	1
1996	Rat	Fire	Feb 19, 1996 - Feb 6, 1997	4	2
1997	Ox	Fire	Feb 7, 1997 - Jan 27, 1998	3	3
1998	Tiger	Earth	Jan 28, 1998 - Feb 15,1999	2	4
1999	Rabbit	Earth	Feb 16, 1999-Feb 4, 2000	1	5
2000	Dragon	Metal	Feb 5, 2000 - Jan 23, 2001	9	6
2001	Snake	Metal	Jan 24, 2001 - Feb 11,2002	8	7
2002	Horse	Water	Feb 12, 2002-Jan 31,2003	7	8
2003	Goat	Water	Feb 1,2003 - Jan 21,2004	6	9
2004	Monkey	Wood	Jan 22, 2004 - Feb 8, 2005	5	1
2005	Rooster	Wood	Feb 9, 2005 - Jan 28, 2006	4	2
2006	Dog	Fire	Jan 29, 2006-Feb 17 2007	3	3
2007	Pig	Fire	Feb 18, 2007 - Feb 6, 2008	2	4
2008	Rat	Earth	Feb 7, 2008 - Jan 25, 2009	1	5
2009	Ox	Earth	Jan 26, 2009 - Feb 13, 2010	9	6
2010	Tiger	Metal	Feb 14, 2010-Feb 2, 2011	8	7
2011	Rabbit	Metal	Feb 3, 2011 - Jan 22, 2012	7	8
2012	Dragon	Water	Jan 23, 2012-Feb 9, 2013	6	9
2013	Snake	Water	Feb 10, 2013-Jan 30, 2014	5	1
2014	Horse	Wood	Jan 31,2014-Feb 18, 2015	4	2
2015	Goat	Wood	Feb 19, 2015-Feb 7, 2016	3	3

2016	Monkey	Fire	Feb 8, 2016-Jan 27,2017	2	4
2017	Rooster	Fire	Jan 28, 2017-Feb 15, 2018	1	5
2018	Dog	Earth	Feb 16, 2018-Feb 4, 2019	9	6
2019	Pig	Earth	Feb 5, 2019 - Jan 24, 2020	8	7
2020	Rat	Metal	Jan 25, 2020 - Feb 11,2021	7	8
2021	Ox	Metal	Feb 12, 2021 - Jan 31,2022	6	9
2022	Tiger	Water	Feb 1,2022-Jan 21,2023	5	1
2023	Rabbit	Water	Jan 22, 2023 - Feb 9, 2024	4	2
2024	Dragon	Wood	Feb 10, 2024-Jan 28, 2025	3	3
2025	Snake	Wood	Jan 29, 2025-Feb 16, 2026	2	4
2026	Horse	Fire	Feb 17, 2026 - Feb 5, 2027	1	5
2027	Goat	Fire	Feb 6, 2027 - Jan 25, 2028	9	6
2028	Monkey	Earth	Jan 26, 2028 - Feb 12, 2029	8	7
2029	Rooster	Earth	Feb 13, 2029-Feb 2, 2030	7	8
2030	Dog	Metal	Feb 3, 2030 - Jan 22, 2031	6	9
2031	Pig	Metal	Jan 23, 2031 - Feb 10, 2032	5	1
2032	Rat	Water	Feb 11,2032-Jan 30, 2033	4	2
2033	Ox	Water	Jan 31,2033- Feb 18, 2034	3	3
2034	Tiger	Wood	Feb 19, 2034 - Feb 7 2035	2	4
2035	Rabbit	Wood	Feb 8, 2035 - Jan 27, 2036	1	5
2036	Dragon	Fire	Jan 28, 2036 - Feb 14, 2037	9	6
2037	Snake	Fire	Feb 15, 2037- Feb 3, 2038	8	7
2038	Horse	Earth	Feb 4, 2038 - Jan 23, 2039	7	8
2039	Goat	Earth	Jan 24, 2039 - Feb 11,2040	6	9
2040	Monkey	Metal	Feb 12, 2040-Jan 31,2041	5	1

2041	Rooster	Metal	Feb 1, 2041 - Jan 21, 2042	4	2
2042	Dog	Water	Jan 22, 2042 - Feb 9, 2043	3	3
2043	Pig	Water	Feb 10, 2043 - Jan 29, 2044	2	4
2044	Rat	Wood	Jan 30, 2044 - Feb 16, 2045	1	5
2045	Ox	Wood	Feb 17, 2045 - Feb 5, 2046	9	6
2046	Tiger	Fire	Feb 6, 2046 - Jan 25, 2047	8	7
2047	Rabbit	Fire	Jan 26, 2047 - Feb 13, 2048	7	8
2048	Dragon	Earth	Feb 14, 2048 - Feb 1, 2049	6	9
2049	Snake	Earth	Feb 2, 2049 - Jan 22, 2050	5	1
2050	Horse	Metal	Jan 23, 2050 - Feb 11, 2051	4	2
2051	Goat	Metal	Feb 12, 2051 - Jan 31, 2052	3	3
2052	Monkey	Water	Feb 1, 2052 - Feb 18, 2053	2	4
2053	Rooster	Water	Feb 19, 2053 - Feb 7, 2054	1	5
2054	Dog	Wood	Feb 8, 2054 - Jan 27, 2055	9	6

MEANINGS OF THE DIRECTIONS AND LOCATIONS

AUSPICIOUS AND FAVOURABLE

Sheng Chi is your success and prosperity: This is one of the best directions to be facing or located in, for just about everything except for sleeping because it is too busy and overwhelming with lots of ideas forming. You can place your desk to face this direction or have your office and if possible, the front of the house facing this direction. You should also keep this area clear of clutter and brightly lit.

Tien Yi is your health: This is a good direction to be facing or located in if one suffers from illness or health problems. If you are building a new house or renovating, ensure that the stove door is facing this direction if possible.

Nien Yen is romance and relationship: This is a good direction or location to improve relationships, not only between partners, but children also. This can be done by placing the bed so that the head points in this direction, especially the master bed. This is a good place for the bed to be located for those wishing to have children, especially for the male.

Fu Wei is personal development and harmony: This is a good location for life in general. It will not bring about great things in prosperity or if you run a business, but it is a good direction if you want to achieve peace and harmony. This is also a good location in assisting learning for school children.

INAUSPICIOUS AND UNFAVOURABLE

Ho Hai is unlucky: This is mildly unlucky in relation to accidents and misfortune. It can relate to financial problems, frustrations, and difficulties in general. However, it is the least unfavourable of the four inauspicious locations.

Wu Kwei is Five Ghosts: This location can bring about theft, relationship problems, job, and financial difficulties. It can cause arguments with everyone and can also affect life at home, as well as at work. If you are building a home, this is a good place for the toilet to be located as you are flushing these negatives down the toilet.

Liu Sha is Six Killings: This can mean missed opportunities and loss at work, or if you own your own business, it can affect the business as well as the home. It can create accidents, sickness (possibly serious illness) and even legal problems. This is a good location for a toilet or even a linen cupboard or storeroom.

Chueh Ming is total loss: This is the worst of the unfavourable or inauspicious directions. It creates serious losses in all aspects of life, chronic illness, bankruptcy, and loss of wealth. If it is possible, never have the front door facing this direction or the bed facing in this direction. The only good place for this location is the toilet, bathroom and even the kitchen.

SOME THINGS TO NOTE

Sitting facing and bed facing

Sitting facing is when you are sitting down, the direction your face and eyes are pointing. Bed facing is when you are lying down on your bed and you are looking up at the ceiling, where the top of your head is pointing is the bed facing. This is generally your headboard.

House missing sectors

If your Life Destiny Palace sector is absent in a home or building, it signifies a lack of energy in that area, rendering the home unable to provide support. In Period 9, it is crucial for the "South" sector not to be missing in any property due to its significance. Missing sectors in a home, particularly Sheng Qi (life success and prosperity), Tien Yi (health), or Nien Yen (longevity and relationships), are unfavourable conditions to have.

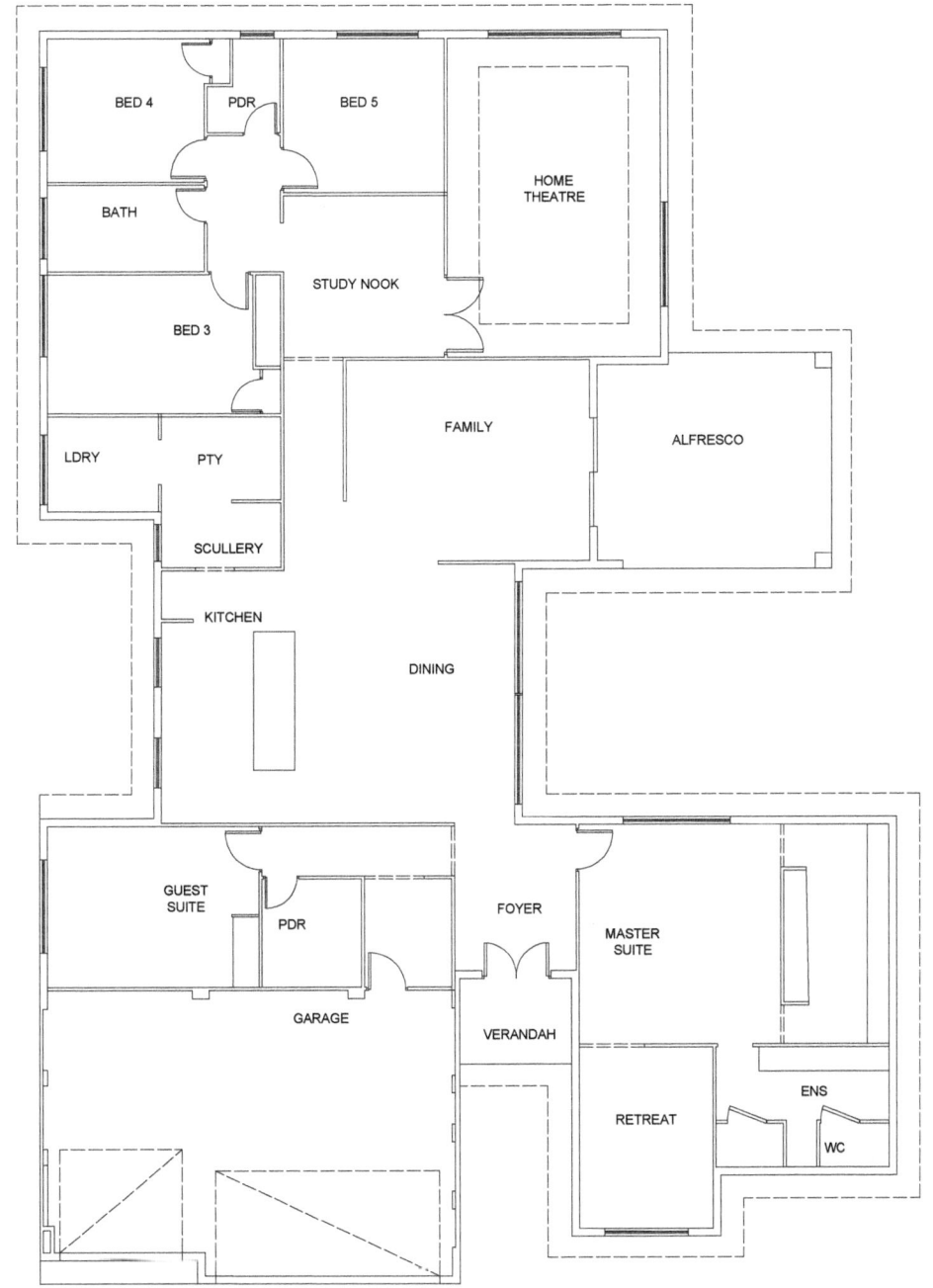

Example of home with missing sectors.

LIFE PALACE DESTINY NUMBER ANALYSIS

NUMBER 1 = WATER

Auspicious directions:

Your Sheng Chi (success and prosperity) direction: Southeast

Your Tien Yi (health) direction: East

Your Nien Yen (romance and relationship) direction: South

Your Fu Wei (personal development and harmony) direction: North

Inauspicious directions:

Your Ho Hai (unlucky) direction: West

Your Wu Kwei (Five Ghosts) direction: Northeast

Your Liu Sha (Six Killings) direction: Northwest

Your Chueh Ming (total loss) direction: Southwest

Number 1 people belong to the [Kan trigram](). They tend to go with the flow. They are extremely flexible and adaptable. Although water people appear calm, quiet, and stable on the outside, they are quite restless on the inside. They love to travel. They hate to be stagnant or stuck in one place. Number 1 people are excellent managers, leaders, and mediators. Overall, water people are charming, courageous, confident, persistent, and liberal. They are deep thinkers. However, diving too deeply into thoughts often makes them sad or depressed. Number 1 people are strong-headed and stubborn. They do not give up easily. They are not afraid of obstacles, and they know how to find their way around problems.

NUMBER 2 = EARTH

Auspicious directions:

Your Sheng Chi (success and prosperity) direction: Northeast

Your Tien Yi (health) direction: West

Your Nien Yen (romance and relationship) direction: Northwest

Your Fu Wei (personal development and harmony) direction: Southwest

Inauspicious directions:

Your Ho Hai (unlucky) direction: East

Your Wu Kwei (Five Ghosts) direction: Southeast

Your Liu Sha (Six Killings) Direction: South

Your Chueh Ming (total loss) Direction: North

Number 2 person is an Earth person and are the most loyal individuals among all other numbers. Number 2 people belong to the Kun trigram. There are two types of earth people – soft earth and hard earth. Number 2 people belong to the former group. They are extremely motherly, nurturing, and caring. They are very tolerant and possess an extremely high thirst for knowledge. Number 2 individuals are down-to-earth, practical, and dependable. They are also blessed with good money management skills. On the downside, Number 2 people are extremely sensitive and less expressive. They internalize everything. This often becomes the cause of their emotional suffering.

NUMBER 3 = WOOD

Auspicious directions:

Your Sheng Chi (success and prosperity) direction: South

Your Tien Yi (Health) direction: North

Your Nien Yen (romance and relationship) direction: Southeast

Your Fu Wei (personal development and harmony) direction: East

Inauspicious directions:

Your Ho Hai (unlucky) Direction: Southwest

Your Wu Kwei (Five Ghosts) Direction: Northwest

Your Liu Sha (Six Killings) Direction: Northeast

Your Chueh Ming (total loss) Direction: West

Number 3 people belong to the Zhen trigram. Like Earth, there are two types of wood people – soft wood and solid wood. Number 3 individuals belong to the latter group. They are strong, enduring, vibrant, and impulsive. They hate competition and they hate being told what must be done. Solid wood people are determined, fearless, and persistent. They like their own space. Like a tree, they tower over others. Although some people might feel overwhelmed by them, others feel sheltered in their domineering presence. They are socially active and have many allies. Number 3 people have a good sense of humor. On the downside, they can be extremely egotistic / self-delusional and do not bend easily, as are extremely stubborn.

NUMBER 4 = WOOD

Auspicious directions:

Your Sheng Chi (success and prosperity) direction: North

Your Tien Yi (health) direction: South

Your Nien Yen (romance and relationship) direction: East

Your Fu Wei (personal development and harmony) direction: Southeast

Inauspicious directions:

Your Ho Hai (unlucky) direction: Northwest

Your Wu Kwei (Five Ghosts) direction: Southwest

Your Liu Sha (Six Killings) direction: West

Your Chueh Ming (total loss) direction: Northeast

Number 4 people belong to the Xun trigram, Life number 4 individuals are soft wood people. They are much more compromising than their unbending Kua 3 counterparts. Soft wood people are extremely instinctive. They are cautiously optimistic and take great care in how they present themselves. They are flexible, romantic, and social. Number 4 individuals are great communicators. They learn faster than others and they know their way to the top. They have a diverse network of friends. Soft wood people like to be independent and, thus, make good entrepreneurs. On the downside, Number 4 people can be very manipulative with words. Also, they are highly emotional and moody. They tend to bend the rules to suit their needs.

Number 5 is the master number in Classical Feng Shui. It is a mixture of both soft earth and hard earth. Hence, Number 5 people have the characteristics of both Number 2 and Number 8. Number 5 people are extremely difficult to understand and cope with. They are the least predictable creatures. If you are a Number 5 person, refer to the description under Number 2 and Number 8. You are a mixture of both. Only you know what you are. Also, you tend to switch roles between soft earth and hard earth. Sometimes you are a flame that provides warmth and sometimes you are the fire that burnt down the city.

NUMBER 6 = METAL

Auspicious directions:

Your Sheng Chi (success and prosperity) direction: West

Your Tien Yi (health) direction: Northeast

Your Nien Yen (romance and relationship) direction: Southwest

Your Fu Wei (personal development and harmony) direction: Northwest

Inauspicious directions

Your Ho Hai (unlucky) Direction: Southeast

Your Wu Kwei (Five Ghosts) Direction: East

Your Liu Sha (Six Killings) Direction: North

Your Chueh Ming (total loss) Direction: South

Number 6 people belong to the Qian trigram and to the hard metal group. They possess high leadership qualities. They are headstrong and obstinate. Number 6 people are strict disciplinarians and are extremely dominating. They are uncompromising and are hard to have a good relationship with. Hard metal people are immensely proud, purposeful perfectionists. Unbending, and extremely focused. They are too conscious about their image in society and will not do anything that would mar their stellar reputation. However, their hardness often causes loneliness and depression. Number 6 people need to learn how to take things easy.

NUMBER 7 = METAL

Auspicious directions:

Your Sheng Chi (success and prosperity) direction: Northwest

Your Tien Yi (health) direction: Southwest

Your Nien Yen (romance and relationship) direction: Northeast

Your Fu Wei (personal development and harmony) direction: West

Inauspicious directions:

Your Ho Hai (unlucky) direction: North

Your Wu Kwei (Five Ghosts) direction: South

Your Liu Sha (Six Killings) direction: Southeast

Your Chueh Ming (total loss) direction: East

Number 7 people belong to the Dui trigram, a Kua 7 individual is among the soft metal group. Although they appear soft on the outside, they are quite stern on the inside. They are good speakers, getting the point across effectively and efficiently. Soft metal people are also very argumentative. However, they have a sharp tongue, and their words are like double-edged swords. They can be both soothing and slicing. It is hard to judge whether you are being complimented or condemned by them. They love to shine and are bit of a show-off. Unfortunately, their outward beauty causes them to be egoistic and snobbish. Number 7 people are quite cunning and are very private. They like to keep their cards close and will offer only "need to know" information. Their lives are often challenging.

NUMBER 8 = EARTH

Auspicious directions:

Your Sheng Chi (success and prosperity) direction: Southwest

Your Tien Yi (health) direction: Northwest

Your Nien Yen (romance and relationship) direction: West

Your Fu Wei (personal development and harmony) direction: Northeast

Inauspicious directions:

Your Ho Hai (unlucky) direction: South

Your Wu Kwei (Five Ghosts) direction: North

Your Liu Sha (Six Killings) Direction: East

Your Chueh Ming (total loss) Direction: Southeast

Number 8 person belong to the Gen trigram. They belong to the hard earth category. They are extremely focused and enthusiastic individuals. Hard earth people often have a one-track mind and single-minded devotion. They prefer learning from their own mistakes rather than learning from others' experiences. Number 8 people do not budge easily. Their stubbornness is their biggest foible.

They tend to be stable and conservative, mulling things over before making a final decision. Earth people are the most loyal of all the numbers. They are self-sacrificing, putting the needs of others before themselves. Hard earth people can either be your best friend or your biggest enemy.

NUMBER 9 = FIRE

Auspicious directions:

Your Sheng Chi (success and prosperity) direction: East

Your Tien Yi (health) direction: Southeast

Your Nien Yen (romance and relationship) direction: North

Your Fu Wei (personal development and harmony) direction: South

Inauspicious directions:

Your Ho Hai (unlucky) direction: Northeast

Your Wu Kwei (Five Ghosts) direction: West

Your Liu Sha (Six Killings) direction: Southwest

Your Chueh Ming (total loss) direction: Northwest

Number 9 people belong to the Li trigram. Fire people are warm, energetic, affectionate, spontaneous, and happy individuals with an unparalleled zeal for life. Number 9 people are the most enlightened and spiritual among all other numbers. They carry a different aura around them. They are usually on the prettier side. Number 9 people are blessed with intelligence, quick thinking ability, and high grasping power. They also seek fame and respect. They need constant love and pampering. On the downside, they are insecure and dependent. Also, fire people are extremely hot-headed.

PERSONAL SPACE SELECTION

In personal space selection, your knowledge of the Life Palace destiny number Gua/Kua is already valuable. However, to elevate this understanding, you can delve deeper by incorporating the flying star numbers of your home's sleeping and living sectors. It is crucial to consider your Gua number, as it represents your individual energy, or chi, that you bring to the rooms you occupy. Your Gua number determines your lucky directions and locations, which can be utilised in conjunction with flying stars to identify the most favourable rooms for you.

According to traditional texts, each of us possesses our own vital chi presence, and when our personal chi aligns harmoniously with the room we occupy, we can expect an abundance of good fortune.

Analysing whether a room is suitable for someone based on their Gua number is a straightforward process. Simply check if the mountain star or water star empowers and corresponds to your Gua number.

The mountain star (sitting star), which is always on the left side, relates to various aspects such as health, romance, relationships, family, authority, mental attitudes, career, fertility, employees, family status, standing in the community, and family popularity.

On the other hand, the water star (facing star), which is always on the right side, corresponds to money, financial status, growth, business prospects, and career luck. Water represents the potential for wealth and prosperity.

For example, if your Gua number is 2, 5, or 8, you belong to the Earth element. If the room you occupy has a mountain star of 6 or 7, the Metal element of 6 or 7 will deplete the Earth energy of 2, causing you to feel tired and tense in that room. However, if you sleep in a room with a mountain star of 8, it adds Earth energy to you, thereby strengthening your good fortune. Moreover, the combination of 8 and 2 adds up to ten, which brings additional good fortune.

For a person with a Gua number of 2 living in a room with a combination of 5 and 9 stars, with 5 representing the mountain star and 9 representing the water star, the harmony between the Earth numbers 5 and 2 makes it a favourable space for the Gua 2 person, despite the 5/9 combination not being ideal.

To make the most of this guideline, it is essential to observe how your Gua element interacts with the corresponding elements of the mountain and water stars. If the water star element aligns with your Gua element, you can expect good fortune in terms of prosperity. Similarly, if the mountain star element corresponds to your Gua element, your relationships, love life, popularity, health, and social life will be greatly favoured.

Conversely, if the water star number element undermines your Gua element, sleeping in that area will result in financial losses. If it is the mountain star number that undermines your Gua element, sleeping in that sector will cause a loss of energy, health, relationship luck, power, authority, and influence.

EXAMPLE:

1 Water	2 Earth	3 Wood
Water = same	Earth = same	Wood = same
Wood = drain	Metal = drain	Fire = drain
Fire = control	Water = control	Earth = control
Earth = destroy	Wood = destroy	Metal = destroy
Metal = produce	Fire = produce	Water = produce
4 Wood	5 Earth	6 Metal
Wood = same	Earth = same	Metal = same
Fire = drain	Metal = drain	Water = drain
Earth = control	Water = control	Wood = control
Metal = destroy	Wood = destroy	Fire = destroy
Water = produce	Fire = produce	Earth = produce
7 Metal	8 Earth	9 Fire
Metal = same	Earth = same	Fire = same
Water = drain	Metal = drain	Earth = drain
Wood = control	Water = control	Metal = control
Fire = destroy	Wood = destroy	Water = destroy
Earth = produce	Fire = produce	Wood = produce

PERSONALISATION WITH 8 SECTORS OF BA GUA

Customising your living or working space using the 8 sectors allows for alignment with your goals and aspirations. By understanding the unique qualities and energies associated with each sector, you can tailor your environment to support and enhance specific areas of your life. This personalised approach empowers you to create a space that resonates with your desires and helps you achieve what you truly want. Whether you're focusing on career advancement, improving relationships, promoting health and well-being, or fostering creativity, aligning with the appropriate sector enables you to harness supportive energies and maximise your potential for success.

Each sector possesses distinct qualities and actions that can be harnessed for success. Depending on your industry or profession, you can leverage specific sectors to boost your achievements:

West = Persuasion:

Ideal for sales professionals, leaders, speakers, personal trainers, writers, authors, and those skilled in storytelling.

Northwest = Control:

Suited for individuals in accounting or risk management roles.

North = Strategic:

Best suited for strategic thinkers, entrepreneurs, business consultants, and long-term planners.

Northeast = Well-being:

Perfect for professionals in the fields of nutrition, education, counselling, holistic healing, alternative therapies, or spiritual practices.

East = Competitive:

Ignites the competitive spirit and benefits lawyers, bankers, entrepreneurs, athletes, sportspeople, and gamers who strive to conquer and succeed.

Southeast = Innovation:

Favors individuals involved in creative pursuits, arts, graphic design, idea generation, and development.

South = Inspiration:

Centred around self-esteem, hope, confidence, and feeling good. Suitable for those in beauty, luxury, spiritual leadership, or preaching.

Southwest = Sustainability:

Well-suited for professionals working in environmental, social, and governance fields, as well as property and real estate developers or agents.

ACTIVATING THE SECTORS

To activate any of these sectors, it is essential for them to have a view of Mountain or Water externally. This requirement applies regardless of your facing or sitting direction, as well as the front or back of your property. External Feng Shui relies on the presence of Mountain or Water for sector activation.

To activate the sectors of South, West, Northwest, and Northeast, ensure that a mountain is visible. If no natural mountain is in sight, consider having a view from these sectors.

To activate the sectors of North, East, Southeast, and Southwest, ensure that water is visible. If there is no natural water source in sight, consider installing a pond, pool, or water feature.

The 8 sectors of Feng Shui also correspond to different organs of the body and influence overall health. If a sector is missing in your living or working space, it can potentially impact your health and make you more susceptible to illness and weaknesses.

The organs of the body and their corresponding sectors in Feng Shui are as follows:

Lung / Big Intestine: Associated with the West or Southwest sector. If these sectors are missing, it may affect respiratory health and the digestive system.

Heart: Aligned with the South sector. If the South sector is missing, it can potentially impact cardiovascular health and emotional well-being.

Mental: Connected to the North sector. If the North sector is missing, it may influence mental clarity, focus, and cognitive abilities.

Fertility: Related to the North sector as well. If the North sector is missing, it could potentially affect fertility and reproductive health.

Skin: Linked to the Southwest or Northeast sector. If either of these sectors is missing, it may impact the health and condition of your skin.

Ensuring that all these sectors are present and balanced in your living or working environment is important to support optimal health and well-being.

The location and positioning of your home also play a vital role in long-term Feng Shui. While "location is everything" is often emphasised, in addition to external factors, there is another important aspect to consider:

FLYING STARS PERIOD 9 FULFILLMENT

Period 9 fulfillment refers to the ability to harness and integrate the energy of Period 9, regardless of the period in which your house was built. By making your house Period 9 fulfilled, you can invite and embrace the energy of Period 9 into your living space.

One popular method to achieve Period 9 fulfillment is using Flying Stars.

Understanding the Flying Stars of your home allows you to adjust and enhancements to align with the favourable energies of Period 9. This involves identifying auspicious and inauspicious stars in different sectors of your home and implementing appropriate remedies or enhancements to optimise the flow of energy.

As Flying Stars provide a powerful tool for harmonising the energy of your living space and creating a favourable environment for growth, prosperity, and well-being during Period 9.

FLYING STARS FENG SHUI FOR PERIOD 9

Before tapping into the best Flying Stars for Period 9 let's do a brief refresh.

NATAL STAR CHARTS

The natal Flying Star Chart of a building, based on its compass direction, reveals its potential and energy map, like an astrological chart. Activating different sectors with auspicious energy is essential. Proficiency in Feng Shui involves analysing, correcting, and enhancing evolving energies as they change over time. Understanding the essence of Flying Stars and applying its techniques is attainable, even for beginners, with dedication.

THE "STARS"

In Flying Stars Feng Shui, the "stars" are symbolic representations of the numbers 1 to 9, embodying specific energies. These stars have distinct qualities that impact various aspects of life, including wealth, health, relationships, and fame. While not actual celestial bodies, they are linked to the seven real stars of the Big Dipper, reflecting the Chinese culture's deep interest in celestial observations and the movements of the planets.

TIME CYCLES OF FLYING STARS FENG SHUI

Flying Stars Feng Shui incorporates a time dimension aspect rooted in significant time cycles and planetary alignments. These cycles include the 180-year Great Cycle, three 60-year cycles, and nine 20-year "Periods." While our focus in this book is primarily on the "Periods," it's important to note the broader context. The Great Cycle marks the alignment of planets every 180 years, divided into Upper, Middle, and Lower cycles. Each 60-year cycle consists of 20-year "Periods" with unique energies. Period 9, which began on February 4th, 2024, carries its distinctive ruling energy associated with its number.

Cycle	Period	Years	Trigram
Upper	1	1864-1884	Kan
	2	1884-1904	Kun
	3	1904-1924	Chen
Middle	4	1924-1944	Xun/Sun
	5	1944-1964	
	6	1964-1984	Qian/Chien
Lower	7	1984-2004	Dui/Tui
	8	2004-2024	Gen/Ken
	9	2024-2043	Li

LOCATING THE CORRECT STAR CHART

If you want to find the unique Flying Star Chart for a home, you'll need two important pieces of information: the move-in date and the house's facing direction. The facing direction refers to how the structure receives energy from a specific direction, while the move-in date determines which Period the structure belongs to, considering the time cycles involved.

MOVE-IN DATE

The move-in date helps determine the Period of a building.

To determine which Period your property, home or commercial building belongs to, you can use the following information:

If you moved in between February 4th, 1984, and February 3rd, 2004, your home is a Period 7.

If you moved in between February 4th, 2004, and February 3rd, 2024, your home is a Period 8.

An exception for Period 7 homes is if major renovations took place after February 4th, 2004. Major renovations include moving out for at least a month, significant changes to the roof (removal and replacement), interior remodelling, front entrance and door renovations, complete painting inside and outside, kitchen or bathroom remodelling, skylight installation, complete floor replacement, adding a room or an attached garage. Any combination of these changes will result in a major shift in energy, causing your Flying Stars to change. If you made such renovations after February 4th, 2004, and your home was initially in Period 7, it will become a Period 8 chart. If you moved in after 2004 and you renovated, your home became a Period 8 chart.

WHAT YOU NEED TO DO TO BE ABLE TO CHANGE PERIOD OF BUILDING

YOU MUST BE ABLE TO CHANGE HEAVEN LUCK.

In the realm of cosmic trinity, heaven symbolises time, the sky, and wind. During the renovation process, it is essential to keep the property open, allowing the daily influx of wind and light. It is suggested that you must open the centre of the house by creating a hole in the roof and ceiling. This is often very difficult to do and presents limitations, especially when trying to change the age of a multi-story property, house or an apartment.

NEXT YOU MUST BE ABLE TO CHANGE EARTH LUCK.

Comprehensive renovations should encompass all aspects of the house, including removing carpets, curtains, and window dressings, upgrading bathrooms and kitchens, repainting or wallpapering walls, and refreshing cupboards and wardrobes—you need to essentially alter the very essence of the "earth" within the space.

LASTLY, YOU MUST CHANGE THE MAN LUCK.

Man, luck refers to people, since people carry the vital energy of Chi, it is crucial to remove them from the property or home for at least a month, along with all furniture.

How can you tell if the process has changed the Period?

If the house's age remains unchanged after the renovation, the lives of the occupants will likely remain unaffected and the same.

But if the Period has truly changed, it brings about improvements in health, wealth, and overall luck for all.

In my over 20-year experience, I found it is very rare for a buildings energy to truly change Period, but it is possible if you get the heaven, earth, and man luck right.

DETERMINING THE FACING DIRECTION

To determine the facing direction of your home, you'll need a fairly accurate compass or a compass app on your smartphone.

If you did not do this exercise at the beginning of the book, let's do it now.

Stand at the front door if it faces the road, as this is where you'll take your compass measurement. In most cases, more than 80% of homes have their doors facing the road and are in the centre of the house, making it straightforward to determine the compass direction. However, if the door does not face the road, stand in the middle of your front backyard or garden to determine the facing degree. Side doors or angled doors should not be used to measure the facing in this system, even if they seem to face the road.

The general rule for determining the facing is to identify where the most vibrant and active (yang) energy is. Typically, nothing compares to the energy of a street. For those living in apartment buildings or condo complexes, use the main door or entrance as the facing direction.

THE 24 MOUNTAINS

In Classical Feng Shui and Flying Stars, the 360 degrees of the compass are divided into 24 sections or directions, known as the 24 Mountains. Each section consists of

15 degrees and represents a subsector of a main direction. For example, South 1, South 2, and South 3 indicate the entire 45 degrees of the South direction, divided neatly into three subsectors.

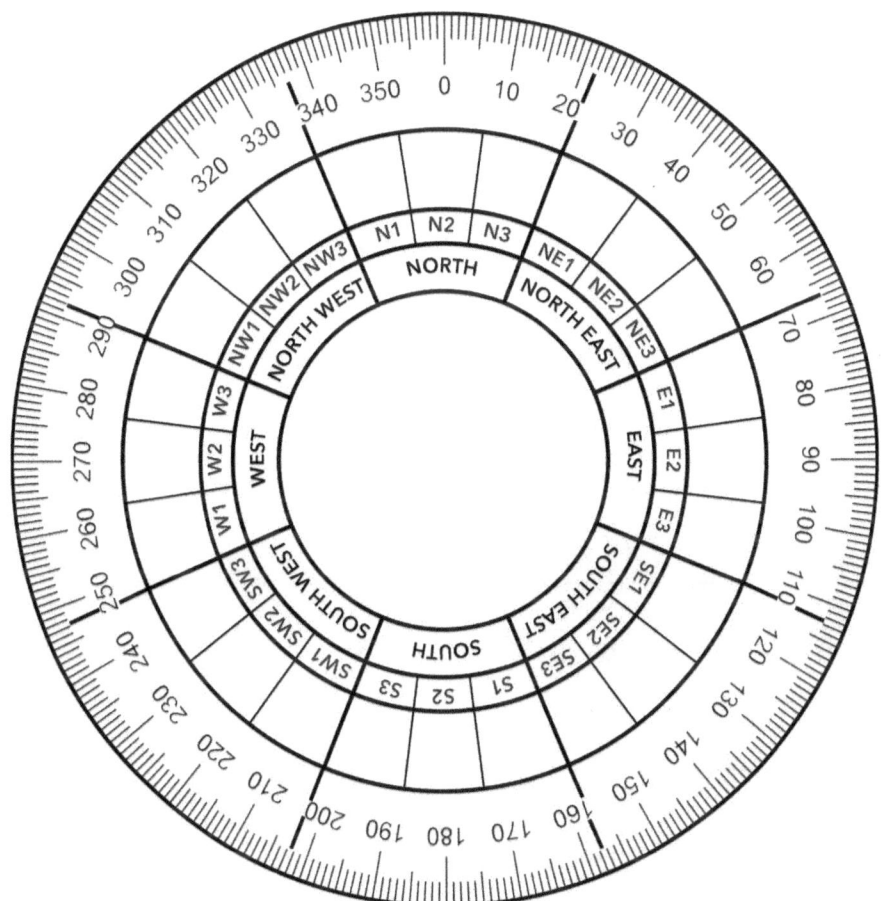

Once you have the exact compass degree, you can find the corresponding subsector on the 24 Mountains Chart. For instance, if your compass reading is 123°, referring to the chart reveals that your structure faces Southeast 1. Similarly, a compass reading of 110 degrees corresponds to East 3. This information is essential whether you're locating the correct Natal Star Chart or planning to fly a Star Chart.

The 24 Mountains Chart indicates the general direction (North, South, East, etc.) and the sub-sector with the exact degree range (S1, E2, NW1, etc.). Once you determine the facing degree, you can refer to this chart for further details.

General	Sub Sector	Compass Degrees	Energy
SOUTH	S1	157.6-172.5	Yang Fire
	S2	172.6-187.5	HORSE
	S3	187.6-202.5	Yin Fire
SOUTHWEST	SW1	202.6-217.5	GOAT
	SW2	217.6-232.5	Earth
	SW3	232.6-247.5	MONKEY
WEST	W1	247.6-262.5	Yang Metal
	W2	262.6-277.5	ROOSTER
	W3	277.6-292.5	Yin Metal
NORTHWEST	NW1	292.6-307.5	DOG
	NW2	307.6-322.5	Metal
	NW3	322.6-337.5	PIG
NORTH	N1	337.6-352.5	Yang Water
	N2	352.6-7.5	RAT
	N3	7.6-22.5	Yin Water
NORTHEAST	NE1	22.6-37.5	OX
	NE2	37.6-52.5	Earth
	NE3	52.6-67.5	TIGER
EAST	E1	67.6-82.5	Yang Wood
	E2	82.6-97.5	RABBIT
	E3	97.6-112.5	Yin Wood
SOUTHEAST	SE1	112.6-127.5	DRAGON
	SE2	127.6-142.5	Wood
	SE3	142.6-157.5	SNAKE

COMPONENTS OF A FLYING STAR CHART

As a Flying Star chart is a simplified energy map of a building that indicates its potential for auspicious or negative events. It consists of three numbers arranged in a nine-square grid, resembling the Luo Shu. Here are the key components of a Flying Star Chart:

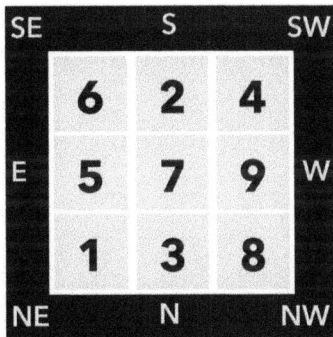

FACING STAR

These numbers, also known as water stars, are in the upper right-hand corner of each palace in the chart. They influence money, financial status, growth, business prospects, and career luck. Facing stars symbolise wealth potential and prosperity prospects. Auspicious facing stars in important areas can bring significant wealth, while unfavourable facing stars indicate potential money loss.

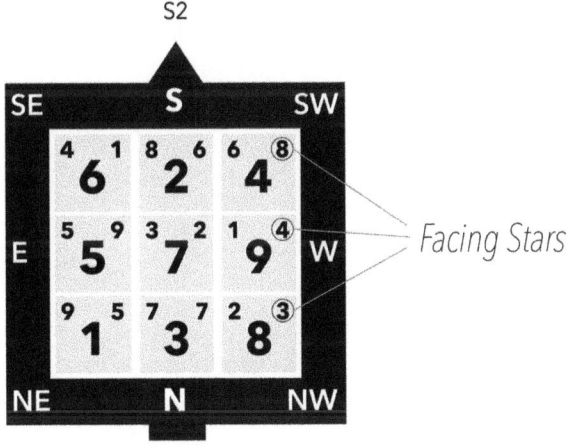

MOUNTAIN STAR

These numbers, also known as sitting stars, are in the upper left-hand corner of each palace in the chart. Mountain stars influence health luck, romance, relationships, family, authority, mental attitudes, career, fertility, and employees. They also represent social status and popularity within the community and family.

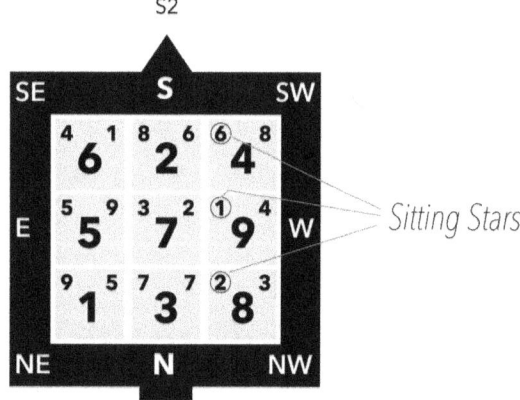

TIME STAR

The time star is a single star located below the facing and mountain stars in each palace of the chart. Unlike facing and mountain stars, time stars are not activated individually. They indicate the Period to which the chart belongs and have the least influence among the three stars.

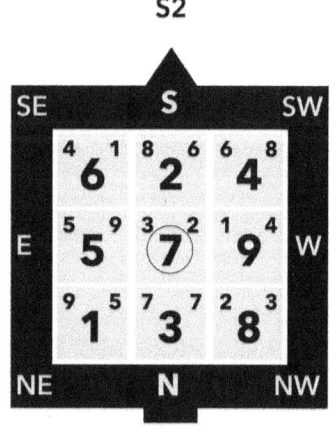

Time Star

Period 1 Flying Star Chart

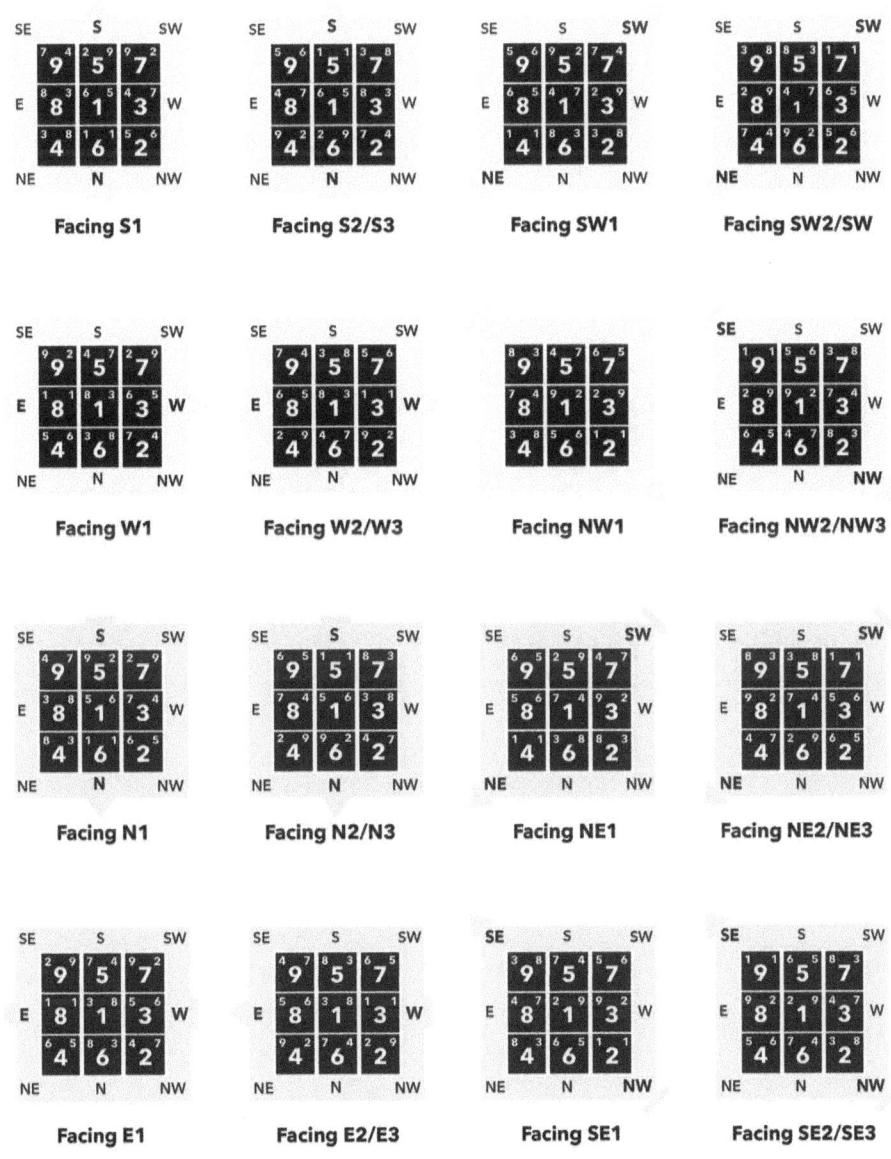

Property built during 1864-1884

Period 2 Flying Star Chart

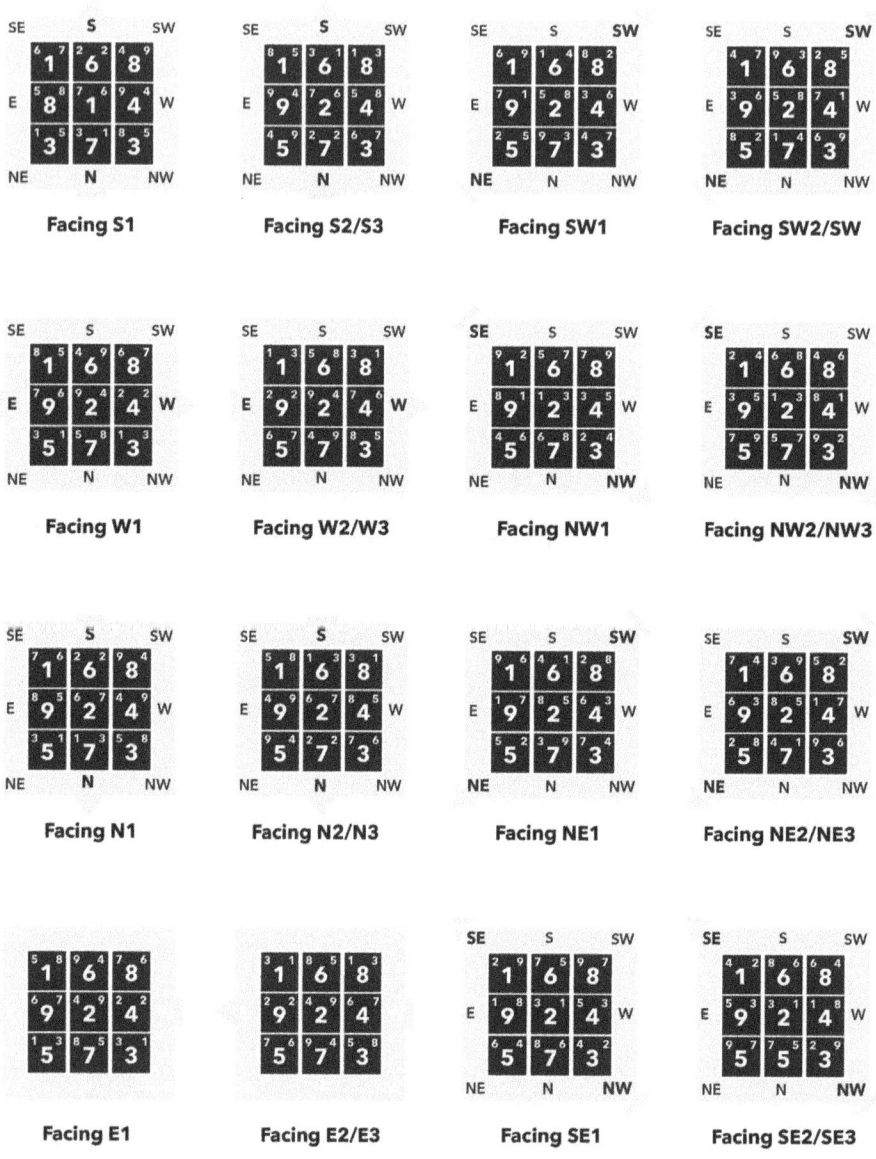

Property built during 1884-1904

Period 3 Flying Star Chart

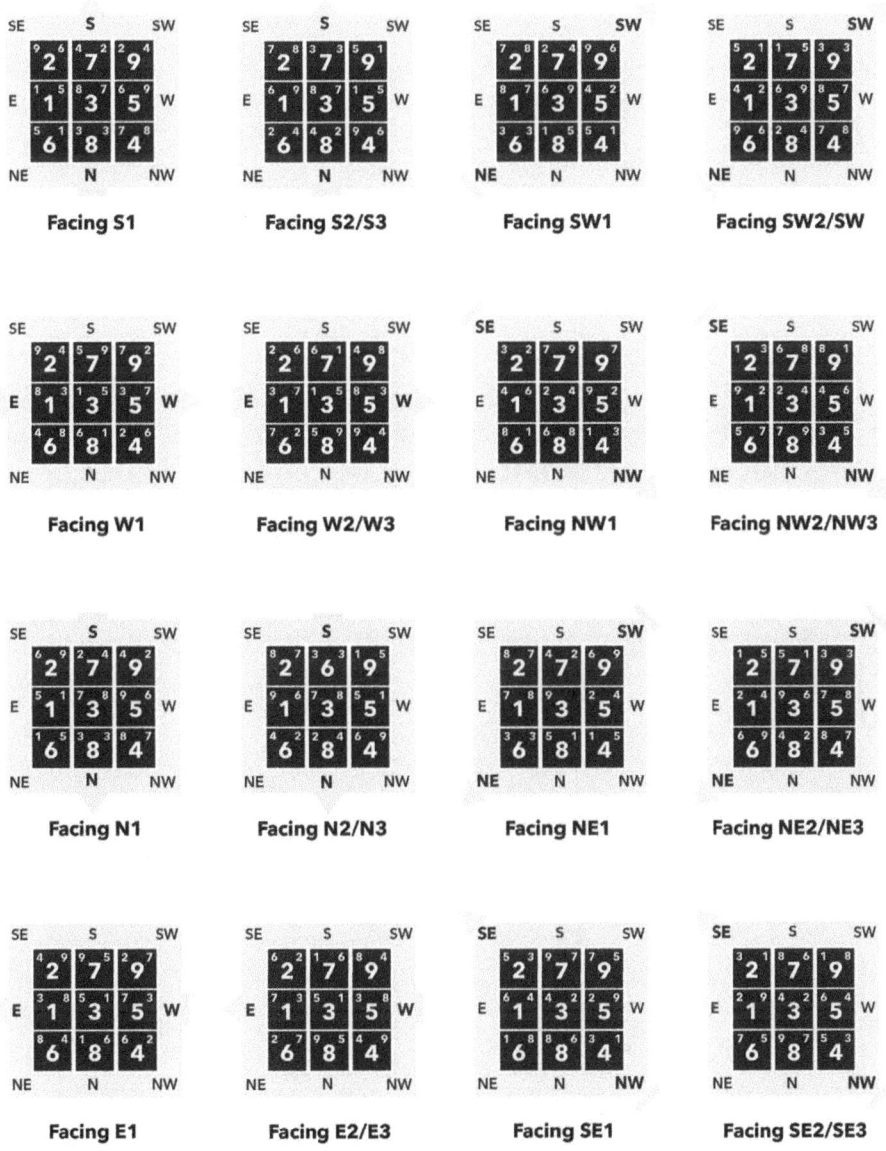

Property built during 1904-1924

Period 4 Flying Star Chart

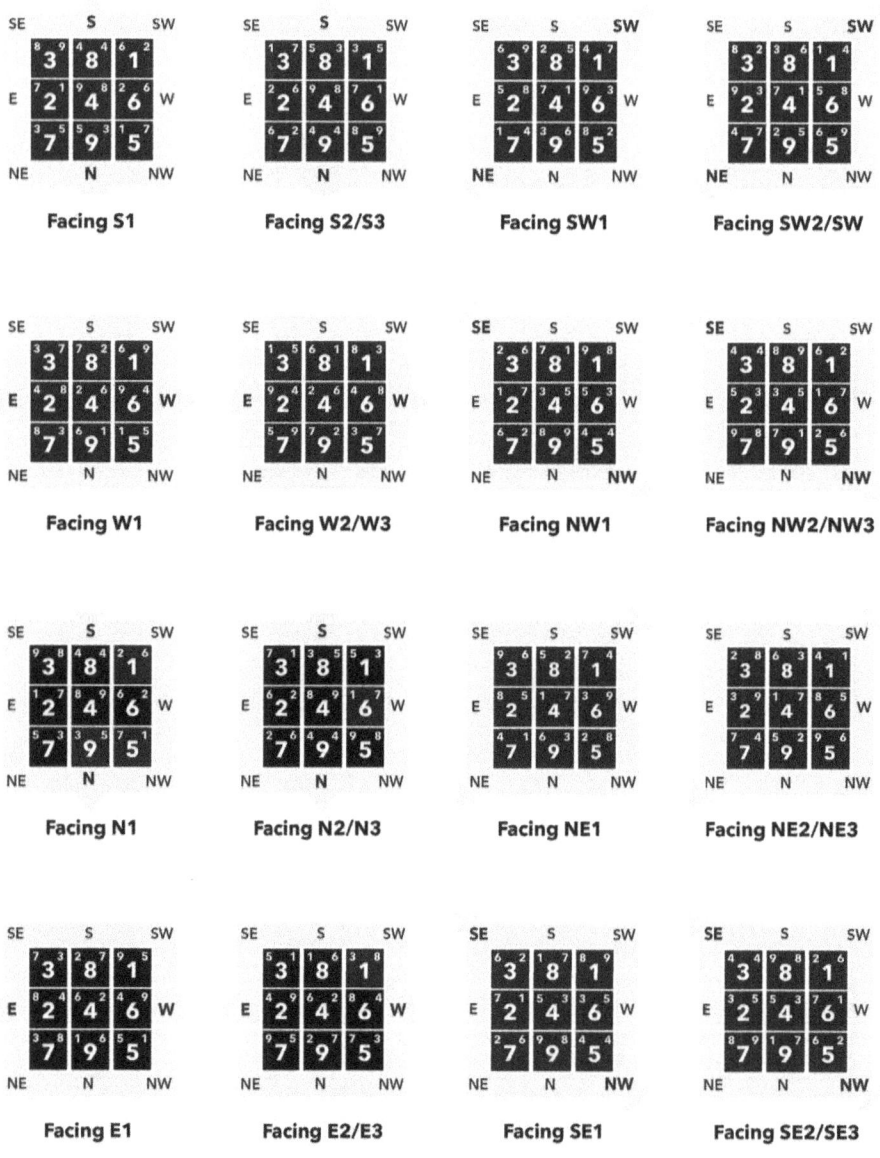

Property built during 1924-1944

Period 5 Flying Star Chart

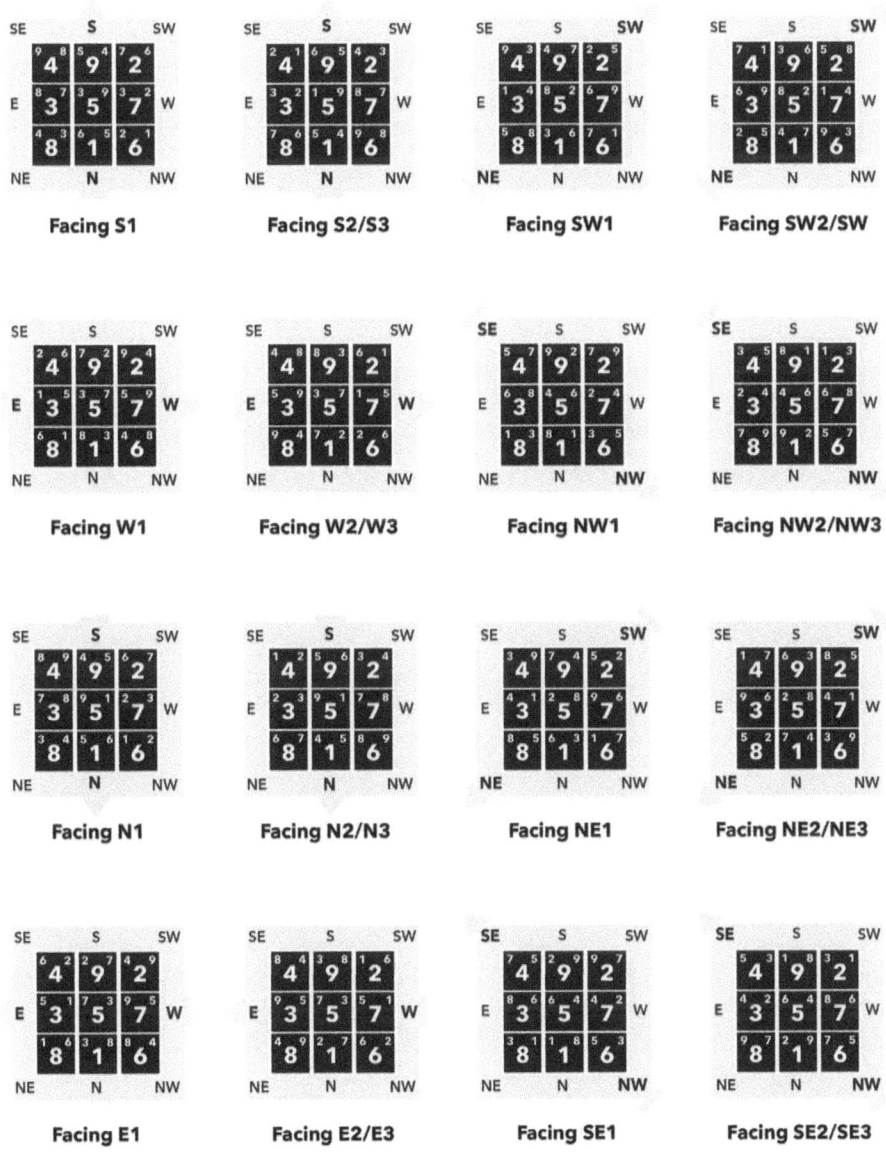

Property built during 1944-1964

Period 6 Flying Star Chart

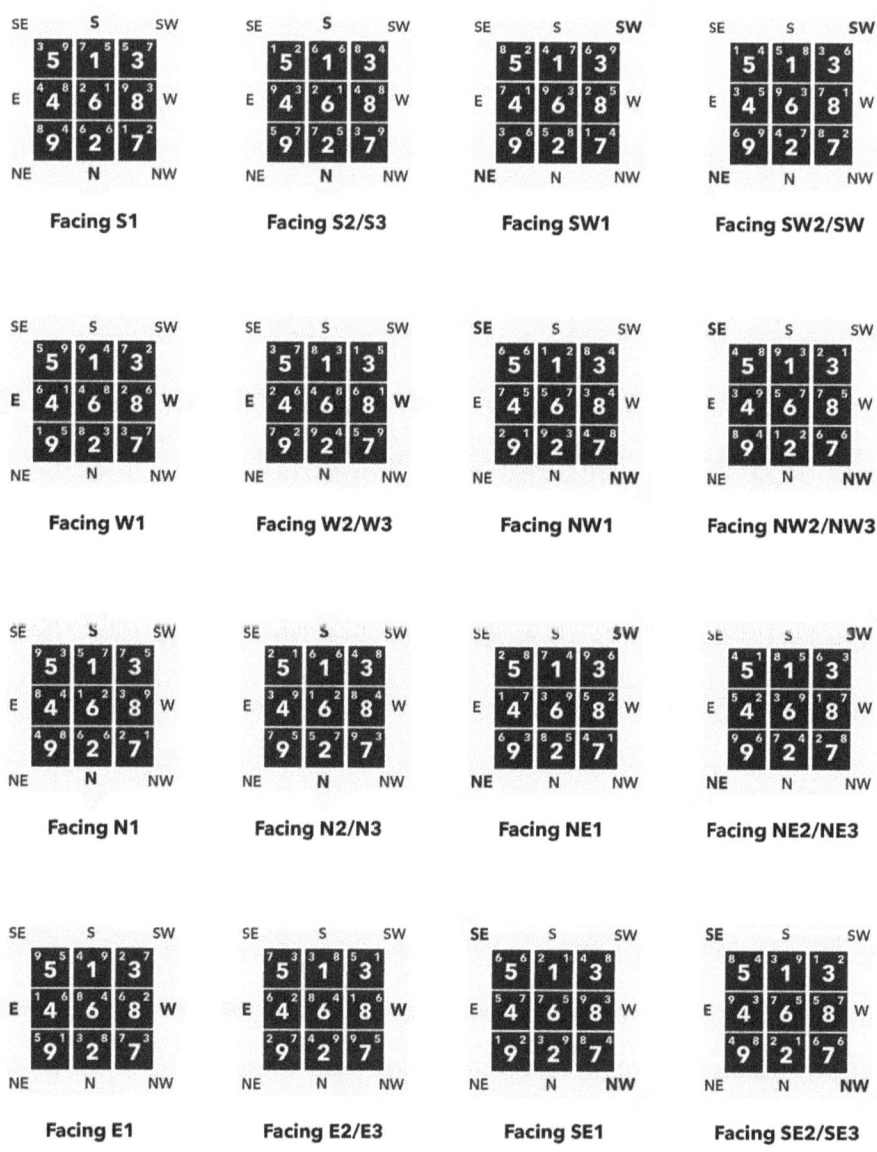

Property built during 1964-1984

Period 7 Flying Star Chart

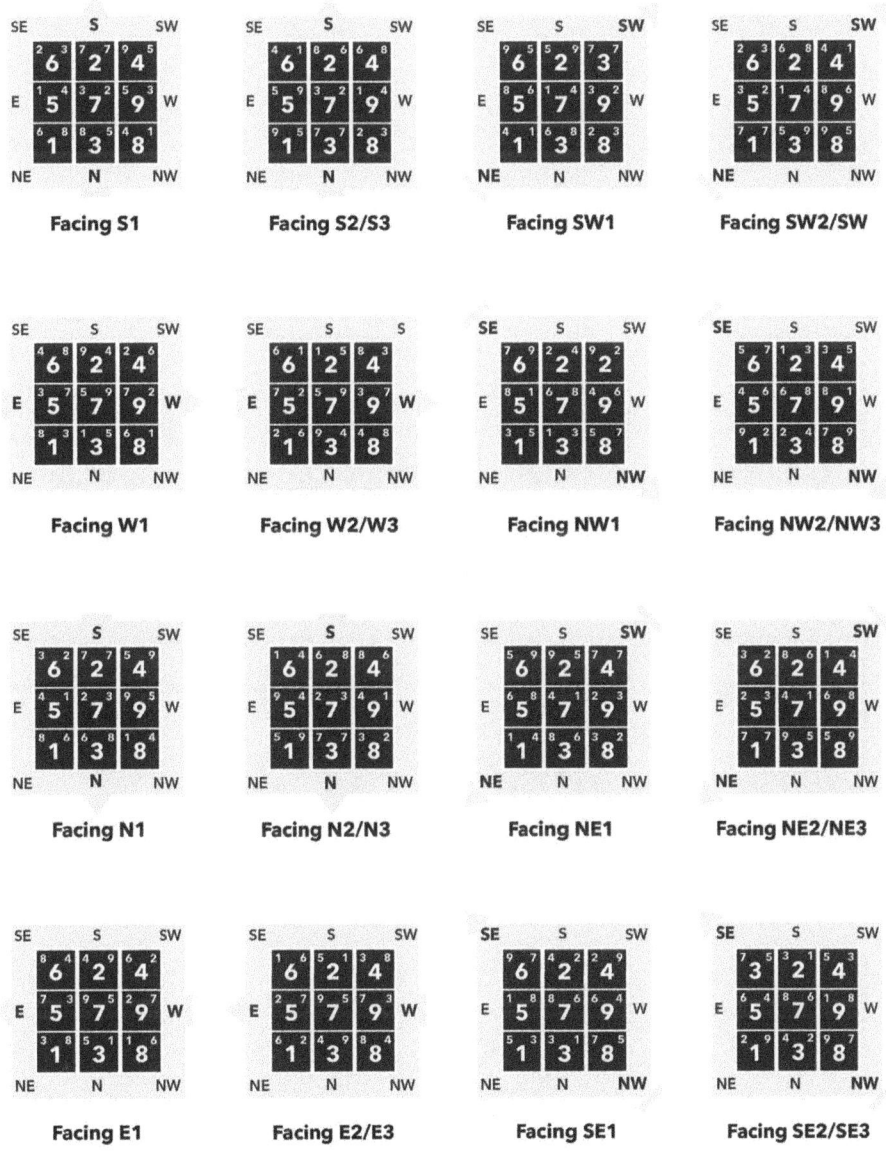

Property built during 1984-2004

Period 8 Flying Star Chart

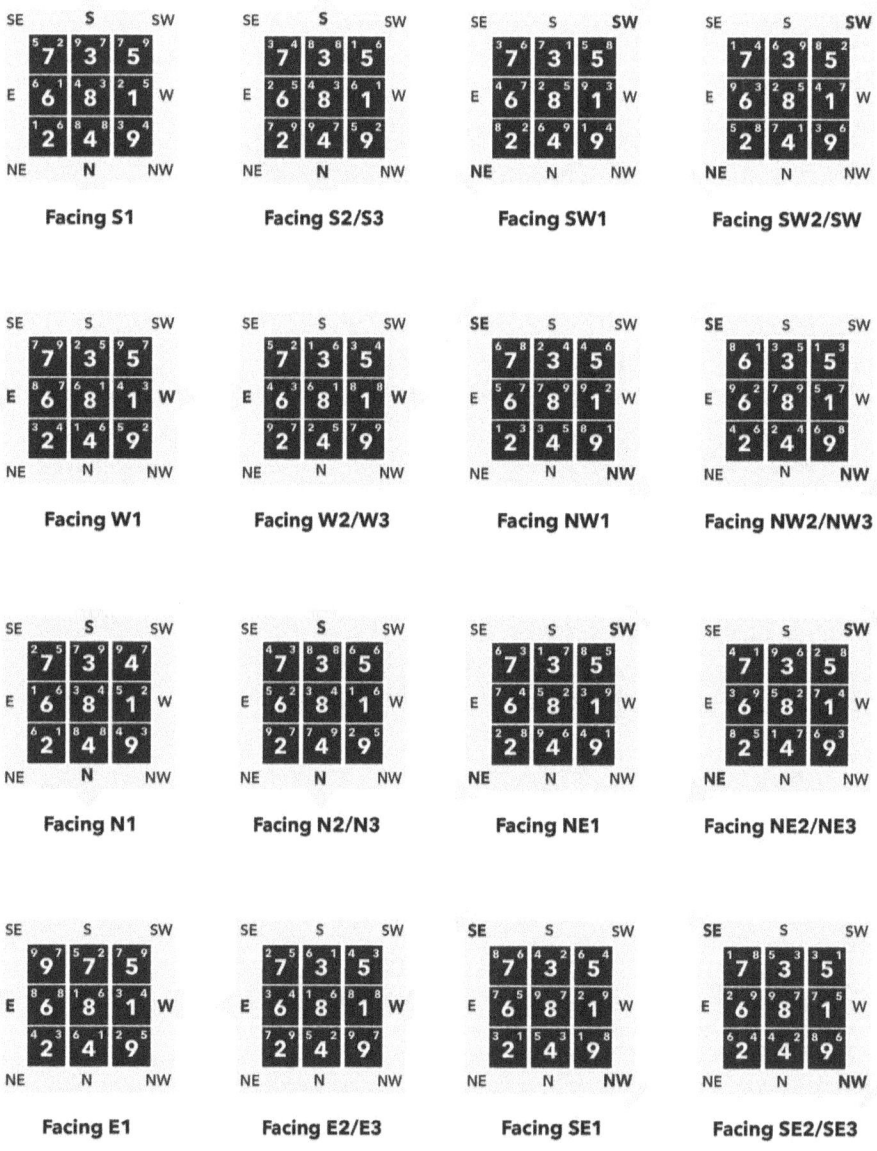

Property built during 2004-2024

Period 9 Flying Star Chart

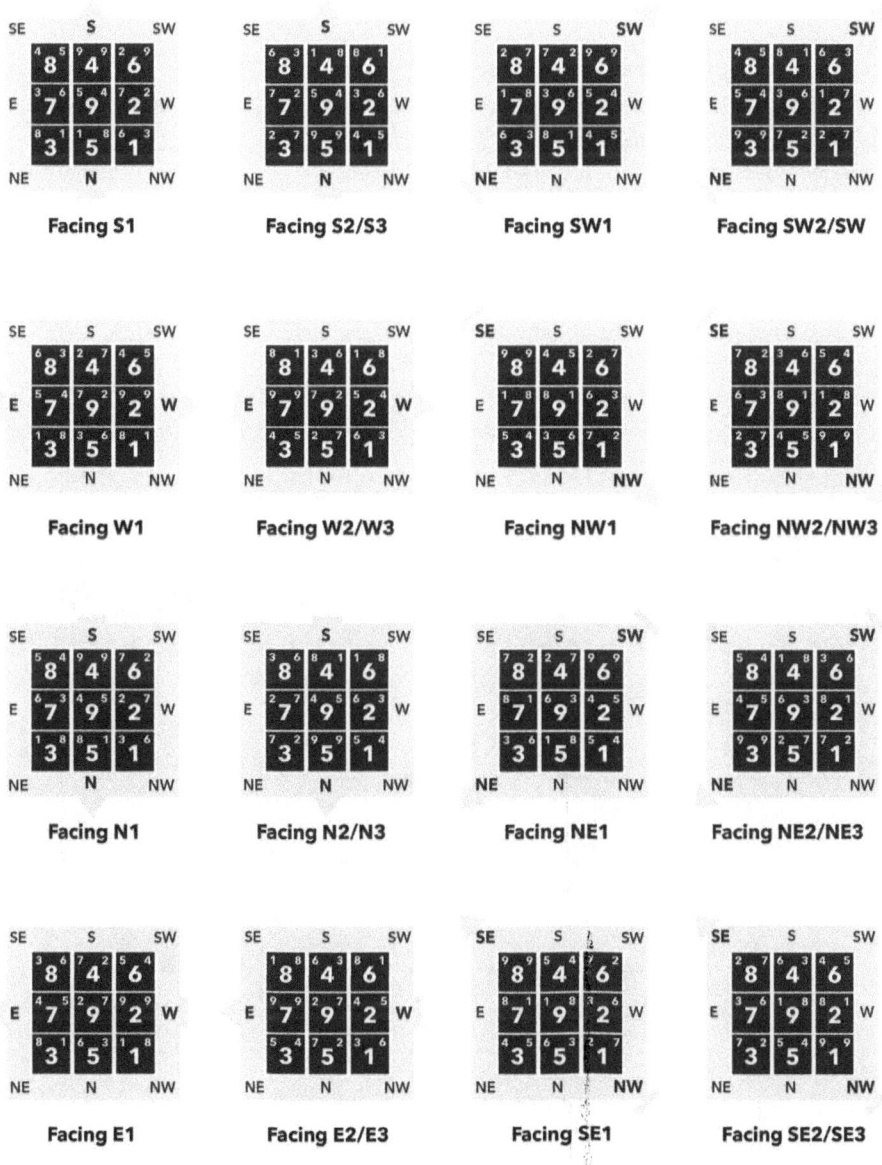

Property built during 2024-2044

There are special charts that time stars can gain significance in such as the Pearl and Parent Strings and the Combination of Ten charts.

PEARL STRING

The "pearl string" refers to a specific configuration of Flying Stars in a natal chart or a specific Period. It is a highly auspicious arrangement that symbolises a string of precious pearls, representing abundance, prosperity, and good fortune. The pearl string formation occurs when the numbers 6, 7, 8, and 9 are arranged in a consecutive pattern within the Flying Star chart. This arrangement signifies a harmonious flow of positive energy, attracting wealth, success, and favourable opportunities. The pearl string is believed to bring forth a continuous stream of auspicious energy, enhancing the overall prosperity and abundance of a space. It is considered a highly desirable configuration, and its activation and enhancement are sought after to harness its positive influences and support the occupants' financial well-being and success.

PARENT STRING

The "parent string" refers to a specific arrangement of Flying Stars in a natal chart or a specific Period that holds significant importance in the practice. The parent string configuration consists of the numbers 1, 4, and 6 aligned consecutively within the Flying Star chart. This arrangement symbolises the nurturing and supportive energy of a parent, providing stability, protection, and guidance. The parent string formation is associated with the qualities of wisdom, authority, and strong foundations. It is believed to bring a sense of security, strength, and solid familial relationships to the occupants of a space. Activating and enhancing the parent string is thought to foster a harmonious and nurturing environment, promoting familial bonds, personal growth, and overall well-being. This configuration is highly valued for its positive influence on family dynamics, stability, and emotional support within a home or workspace.

COMBINATION OF TEN

The "combination of ten" is a significant configuration that arises from the arrangement of Flying Stars in a natal chart or a specific Period. It involves the interaction and combination of the numbers 1 through 9, along with a special "extra" star, often represented by the number 10. The combination of ten represents a harmonious and balanced energy field where all the stars work together in synergy to enhance the auspicious qualities and potentials of a space. This configuration signifies a state of completeness, wholeness, and favourable circumstances. The combination of ten is believed to bring forth abundance, success, and overall positive outcomes in various aspects of life, including wealth, relationships, career, and health. Activating and maximising the potential of the combination of ten is considered highly auspicious, as it aligns the energies in a space to support and manifest desired outcomes. This configuration is highly sought after for its ability to create a harmonious and prosperous environment that promotes overall well-being and success.

In the nine-celled grid, each "box" is referred to as a palace, sector, or direction interchangeably.

GOOD AND BAD STARS:

To understand Flying Stars fully, it's essential to know the meaning of each star and its implications. In this system, the good stars are 1, 2, 6, 8, and 9, whether they are facing or mountain stars. The 4 star represents romance, travel, writing, publishing, scholarly pursuits, fame, and supports those with a public persona. The 3 star is more favourable in Period 9, indicating progressive energy rather than lawsuits and robbery. However, it Requires to be paired with a good star to be interpreted as such.

Conversely, the 5, and 7 stars are considered bad stars. The 5 star is the most negative and associated with various disasters. Bad stars are only considered advantageous within their respective Periods (20-year increments). For example, the 5 star is only beneficial in Period 5. The same applies to the 3, and 7 stars.

ACTIVATING THE STARS:

Different energy, objects, or activities are required to activate the facing stars compared to the mountain stars. To amplify the positive energy of facing stars, one can use a well-used door or moving water such as a fountain. Mountain stars, on the other hand, require stillness or objects that emulate the height and weight of a mountain, such as brick or stone courtyard wall, heavy stone or concrete pots, planters, or boulders.

The facing and mountain stars hold the most importance in the Flying Star chart, with the facing ruling star (9 facing star in Period 9) being the most significant. The time stars are not individually activated but play a crucial role in specialised star charts like the Combination of Ten, Pearl and Parent Strings.

Understanding how to activate or deactivate the stars is important for maximising positive energy and minimising negative influences in a property.

HOW TO GET THE STARS ACTIVATED

So how is best to activate the Mountain and Facing Stars?

MOUNTAIN STARS:

Mountain stars in a Flying Star chart can be activated through stillness or objects that emulate the height and weight of mountains.

Here are some various ways to activate mountain stars:

Natural mountains or hills,

Landscape mounds (as found on golf courses),

Sleep (referring to the stillness and stability of the sleeping environment),

Retaining walls,

Brick or stone walls,

Landscape boulders,

Courtyard walls,

Pergolas, gazebos, or pagodas,

Staircases,

Fireplace locations,

Stoves (which have substantial weight),

Tall or solid cabinets,

Large pots or planters,

Tall, heavy bookcases,

Anything exterior that is 3 feet or taller.

FACING STARS:

Facing stars, on the other hand, require activity or objects that represent movement.

Here are some different methods to activate facing stars:

Real water such as pool, ponds, streams, or the ocean,

Virtual water such as roads, driveways, and pathways,

Doors, including front, back, and interior garage doors,

Water Features or Fountains, whether indoors or outdoors,

Low ground areas like natural washes or sloping land,

Real fire sources like fireplaces, stove locations, or fire pits,

Canals,

Waterfalls, including man-made ones,

Stove knobs, buttons, or controls,

Oven and microwave doors,

Outdoor fireplace openings,

Pizza oven openings,

Electronic devices like TVs, computers, and electrical towers.

These activation methods are used to enhance the energy and influence of the mountain and facing stars in a Flying Star chart, either by creating stillness or by introducing activity and movement.

STEP 1 FOR PERIOD 9 FENG SHUI FULFILLMENT

To enhance the internal Feng Shui of your home, follow these steps:

Identify the Number "9":

In your Flying Star chart, you (will be able to locate your Flying Star chart on pages 137-145), locate the small numbers associated with each sector.

Look for the number "9," as it represents the Flying Star energy of Period 9.

Focus on the Flying Star "9" Location:

Try spending more time in the sector of your home where the Flying Star "9" is present.

This sector is considered auspicious and holds the energy associated with Period 9.

By emphasising the Flying Star "9" location and spending more time there, you can tap into the positive energy of Period 9 and enhance the internal Feng Shui of your home.

If you cannot spend time in the "9" sector, look for the "1" sector and utilise its energy.

STEP 2 FOR PERIOD 9 FENG SHUI FULFILLMENT

To optimise the Feng Shui of your home, consider the following steps:

Identify Key Areas:

Pay attention to important areas of your home, such as the main door, bedroom, balcony, study/office, and storage/kitchen spaces. These areas have a significant impact on the overall energy flow within your living environment.

Locate the Flying Star "9" or "1":

Determine the best position for the Flying Star "9" or "1" within your home. These Flying Stars represent auspicious energies associated with Period 9. By having either of these Flying Stars present in the designated areas, you can enhance the positive energy and create a harmonious environment.

By focusing on these key areas and ensuring the presence of the Flying Star "9" or "1," you can align your home with the beneficial energies of Feng Shui and promote a sense of balance and well-being in your living space.

STEP 3 SELECTIVE FULFILLMENT

In Period 9, enhancing prosperity and auspicious energies in your building can be achieved by locating Water and Mountain Stars.

AREA SITTING STAR FACING STAR

AREA	SITTING STAR *(LEFT)*	SITTING STAR *(RIGHT)*
MAIN DOOR		9,1
BEDROOM	9,1	
KITCHEN		9,1,3,4
STUDY ROOM		9,1
BALCONY		9,1

The influence of Flying Star 2 in Period 9 may take time to manifest, so its effects may not be immediately noticeable. It's important to remember that the power of a specific sector in your space holds more significance than the overall directional alignment.

Now that you have assessed the overall fulfillment for Period 9, the next step is to focus on the location and activation of your space.

CHARTS AND ACTIVATION OF PERIOD 9

PREPARING FOR PERIOD 9

As of February 4, 2024, Period 9 begins, marking a significant change in Feng Shui energy worldwide. To get started and determine your unique chart, you'll need to know the facing direction of your home. Remember your move-in date determines the Period your house falls into.

Refer to your chart and time Period on pages 137-145.

If you haven't yet, draw a floor plan of your home and divide it into nine sectors, overlaying the directions.

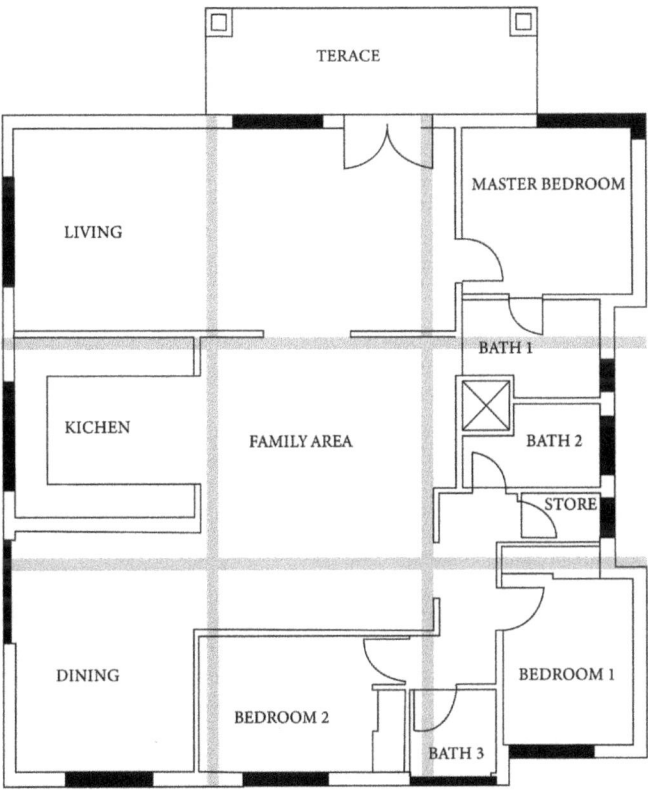

Now superimpose or place your charts information in the corresponding sectors.

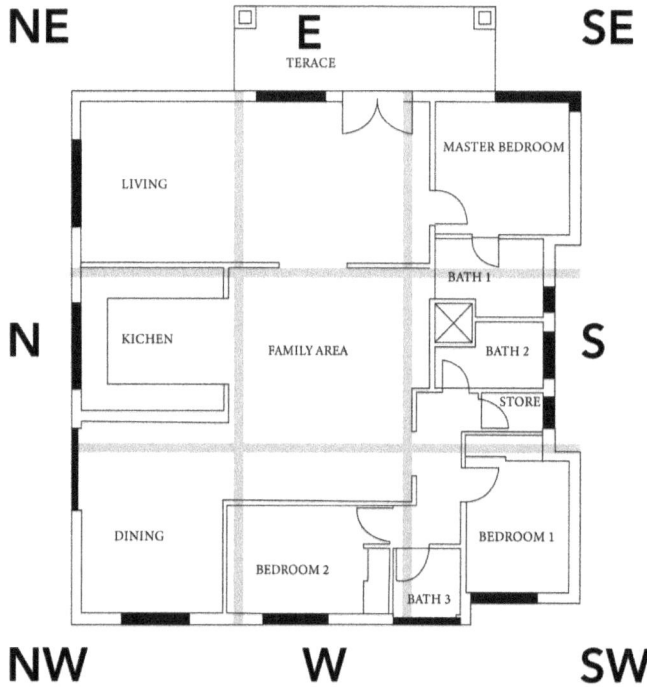

You may now want to sketch in potential bed locations, desks, water placements, and other elements as you read the recommendations, on to your plan.

Only one chart applies to your home and its unique energy, while the other charts serve as helpful references for your friends, family, co-workers, or future homes.

Mastering Flying Stars takes time, as well as the other Feng Shui systems. However, the charts have been fully evaluated for your convenience. (refer to pages 137-145 for chart)

The following recommendations and assessments incorporate the five elements, cosmic trinity, timeliness of the stars, annual stars, proper activation of mountain and facing stars, He Tu, Luo Shu, the two Ba gua's, Eight Mansions, and Flying Stars formulas. The recommended enhancements and cures in the charts are necessary to unlock the full potential and ensure the most positive energy.

A COUPLE OF INTERESTING FACTS ABOUT PERIOD 9 CHARTS

All Period 9 charts have double 9's either in the front or back.

In Period 9, there are two unique Combination of Ten charts located on the Southeast 2/3 and Northwest 2/3 facings. Additionally, in every palace of the charts, except for the front and back ones, the mountain and facing stars combine to form a total of 9. This creates harmonious combinations of stars, but it also introduces negative combinations that require remedial measures.

It's important to remember that Feng Shui considers both location and direction, making the most of both location and direction is beneficial, for the most powerful results.

BEST ACTIVATION FOR PERIOD 9 PROPERTY

For the best long-term luck of a property and the best compliance for Period 9 it is best to start with the external landforms being Water and Mountains or Hills. Once you are aware of the facing direction of your property you can fine tune your external and then internal environment to make the most of your property.

PERIOD 9

South 1 (157.6° to 172.5°)

External outdoor activation

Water and Mountain required in the front.

The South 1 facing property, has the double 9's at the front of the chart. South 1-facing structures are beneficial for people in positions of authority, as well as for families looking to accumulate property. It can also attract descendants who will achieve high-ranking political positions. To fully harness the positive energy and activate health, wealth, and harmony, it is recommended to place a large water feature, such as a stone fountain, a pond, or waterfall, in the front of the home. Additionally, incorporating a 'mountain' element is important, which can be achieved through landscaping mounds, boulders, courtyard walls, tall and heavy planter pots, pillars, stone/brick fireplaces, or other tall and substantial objects made of earth materials near the front entrance. It's worth noting that trees do not serve as a representation of a mountain. For those residing in apartments, high-rise buildings, townhouses, condominiums, or rented spaces where outdoor water features are not feasible, placing a water feature indoors in the recommended area can still activate the energy. Similarly, to activate the mountain element in the recommended area, tall furniture like a cupboard or wardrobe or heavy bookcases, as well as stone statues, can effectively enhance the energy.

Regarding the back of your property, if you want to achieve positive results, place a water feature, a pond, or swimming pool in the North or Northeast sector.

PERIOD 9

South 2 (172.6° to 187.5°)

South 3 (187.6° to 202.5°)

External outdoor activation

Mountain and Water required at the back.

South 2 and 3 facing properties have double 9's at the back of the property, meaning containing the powerful energy of double 9's in the rear, which can bring significant benefits in terms of health, relationships, and finances. To fully activate this chart, it is crucial to incorporate both a mountain and water element. The mountain element can be created using higher ground, landscape mounds, boulders, or a combination of these elements (ensuring at least 3-foot height). At the back of the property, you can place a water feature such as a fountain, a pond, water feature, a pond, or swimming pool. If it is not possible to install an outdoor water feature in your home, you can place an indoor water feature, like a wall fountain, in the recommended area. Similarly, for those residing in apartments, high-rise buildings, townhouses, condominiums, or rented spaces where outdoor water features are not feasible, placing an indoor water feature in the recommended area is a suitable alternative. To activate the mountain element in the recommended area, you can use tall furniture like a cupboard or wardrobe, heavy bookcases, or stone statues, as these items effectively enhance the energy.

When it comes to the back of your property having a water feature, a pond, or swimming pool, for optimal results, is advised to be in the North. However, it is important to ensure that the pool does not touch or reside in the Northwest sector.

PERIOD 9

Southwest 1 (202.6° to 217.5°)

External outdoor activation

The Southwest 1 property boasts the most favourable stars of Period 9, with double 9's at the front of the property. This energy brings exceptional luck and benefits in all aspects of Feng Shui, including prosperity, health, and harmony additionally, Southwest-facing properties have the potential to transform misfortunes into lucrative opportunities and may even signify the birth of an intelligent, wealthy, and prosperous individual. To fully harness this incredible energy, it is essential to incorporate both a water feature and a mountain element in the front garden. The mountain element can be created using higher ground, courtyard walls, landscape mounds, or boulders, either individually or in combination (ensuring it is at least 3 feet high). As for the water feature, it can take the form of a fountain, stream, or Koi Pond. For individuals living in apartments, high-rise buildings, townhouses, condominiums, or rented spaces where outdoor water features are not feasible, placing an indoor water feature in the recommended area is a suitable alternative. To activate the mountain element in the recommended area, you can use tall furniture such as a large wardrobe, heavy bookcases, or stone statues, as these items effectively enhance the energy.

Regarding the back of your property a water feature, a pond, or swimming pool, is best located in the East (right-hand corner) or North (left-hand corner) of the backyard. However, it is important to ensure that the pool does not touch the area between 352.6° to 7.5°, as this may activate extramarital affairs. Additionally, placing water in the Northeast sector could potentially lead to legal disputes, while water located in the Northwest may activate disasters.

PERIOD 9

Southwest 2 (217.6° to 232.5°)

Southwest 3 (232.6° to 247.5°)

External outdoor activation

Install Mountain and Water at the back.

The Southwest 2 and 3 facing property has the prosperity and positive energy at the back, with the energy of double 9's at the back. Southwest-facing properties are renowned for their ability to transform bad luck into profitable opportunities and may even signify the birth of an intelligent, wealthy, and prosperous individual. To properly activate this chart, it is important to incorporate both water and a mountain element at the back of the property. The mountain element can be created using a solid wall or fence made of stucco, brick, or stone. Alternatively, well-designed tiered landscaping or a series of stacked terraces can also serve as an effective mountain feature. When designing this significant element, make sure to include a proportionate water feature in the back of your home and garden. If you live in an apartment, high-rise building, townhouse, condominium, or rented space where an outdoor water feature is not feasible, you can place an indoor water feature at the back of your space, preferably in the east. Additionally, large, and heavy bookcases or wardrobes can represent the mountain element, and they should be placed against the back wall.

Regarding the backyard a water feature, a pond, or swimming pool, is recommended to be in the Northeast (centre) of the backyard. However, placing water in the North could potentially lead to health issues, while water in the Southeast may activate disasters.

PERIOD 9

West 1 (247.6° to 262.5°)

External outdoor activation

Mountain and Water in required in the front.

The West 1 property holds the current prosperity and positive energy, at the front, characterised by the double 9's, meeting at the front or entrance. These West-facing properties tend to nurture well-educated, intelligent, polite, and charming individuals who have the potential to achieve great wealth through effective business management or political involvement. To fully harness the most auspicious energy and activate health, wealth, and harmony, it is recommended to incorporate both water and a mountain element at the front of the home. The water element

can be represented by a large stone fountain, a pond, or waterfall. The mountain element can be created using landscaping mounds commonly found on golf courses, boulders, courtyard walls, tall and heavy planter pots, basalt pillars, stone/brick fireplaces, or any other tall and weighty items made from earth materials. It's important to note that trees do not represent a suitable mountain element. In cases where you reside in an apartment, high-rise building, townhouse, condominium, or rented space where an outdoor water feature is not feasible, you can place an indoor water feature in the recommended area. Additionally, large, and heavy bookcases or wardrobes can serve as a representation of the mountain element, and should be placed against the West wall.

Regarding the rear or backyard of the property a water feature, a pond, or swimming pool, is advisable in the Northeast (left-hand corner) of the backyard. However, water in the East (centre) is beneficial for individuals in professions such as writing, teaching, or those with a public persona. It's important to be cautious as water in this area may lead to extramarital affairs and troubled romantic relationships.

PERIOD 9

West 2 (262.6° to 277.5°)

West 3 (277.6° to 292.5°)

External outdoor activation

Mountain and Water recommended at the back.

The West 2 and 3 properties have current prosperity and highly auspicious energy (represented by the double 9's) found at the back. West-facing homes are known to foster dynamic individuals who can achieve success and accumulate significant wealth at a rapid pace. These properties also support influential politicians, exceptional academic achievements, and outstanding athletes. To fully harness this incredible energy, it is essential to incorporate both a water feature and a mountain element in the backyard. The mountain element can be created using higher ground, courtyard walls, landscape mounds, or boulders, or a combination of these elements, reaching a height of at least 3 feet. Additionally, consider installing a beautiful water feature such as a fountain, stream, or Koi Pond, in the front garden. For those residing in apartments, high-rise buildings, townhouses, condominiums, or rented spaces where outdoor water features are not feasible, placing an indoor water feature in the recommended area is a suitable alternative. To activate the mountain element in the designated area, you can use tall cupboard or wardrobes, heavy bookcases, or stone statues, as these items will effectively stimulate the energy.

For the rear or back of the property a water feature, a pond, or swimming pool, is recommended to be in the East. However, it can also be placed in the Southeast. It is common for pool designs to touch two sectors. However, be cautious not to have water in the Northeast (left-hand corner) of the backyard, as it may activate potential disasters.

PERIOD 9

Northwest 1

External outdoor activation

Mountain and Water required at the back.

The Northwest 1 property benefits from the auspicious arrangement of the Double 9 Stars meeting at the back, with the current prosperity and highly favourable energy (represented by the number 9) located at the back. When the landforms are favourable, Northwest-facing properties have the potential to bring significant wealth to their occupants. To fully harness the incredible potential of this arrangement, it is essential to incorporate both a mountain and water feature at the back of the property. The 'mountain' element can be created using higher ground, landscape mounds, or boulders. Alternatively, a combination of these elements, with a minimum height of 3 feet, can be employed. Smartly designed tiered landscaping or a series of stacked terraces can also be effective in enhancing the aesthetic appeal and energetic flow of the area. To introduce the water element, consider installing a swimming pool, waterfall/a pond, Koi Pond, lake, or spa at the back of the property. These water features not only contribute to a serene ambiance but also activate the positive energy associated with prosperity. For individuals residing in apartments, high-rise buildings, townhouses, condominiums, or rented spaces where outdoor water features are not feasible, it is recommended to place a water feature indoors in the designated area. This could be a stone fountain, a pond, or waterfall that sufficiently represents the water element and supports the flow of positive energy. To activate the mountain energy indoors, you can use a tall cupboard or wardrobe, heavy bookcases, or stone statues strategically placed in the recommended area.

Regarding the backyard swimming pool, if you desire to have one, the ideal location would be the Southeast. However, it can also be placed in the East (left-hand corner) of the backyard. It is important to note that the water should not be

positioned between 82.5° to 97.5° as it may potentially activate affairs. Additionally, it is advised to avoid placing water features in the South (right-hand corner) as this can activate unfavourable energies associated with disasters.

By implementing these recommendations, you can maximise the positive energy flow, attract prosperity, and create a harmonious and auspicious environment on your property.

PERIOD 9

Northwest 2 (307.6° to 322.5°)

Northwest 3 (322.6° to 337.5°)

External outdoor activation

Water and Mountain required at the front.

The Northwest 2 and 3 property is one of the luckiest Period 9 charts with the double 9 flying stars at the front. But each sector also has a combination of ten with water star and natal stars combining to 10. This chart holds great auspiciousness. When the landforms are favourable, Northwest-facing properties have the potential to bring substantial wealth. To properly activate this chart, it is essential to incorporate both water and a mountain element at the front of the property. The water element can take the form of a large stone fountain, a pond, or waterfall. As for the mountain element, it can be created using landscaping mounds, boulders, courtyard walls, tall and heavy planter pots, pillars, stone/brick fireplaces, or other tall and weighty items made of earth materials. It's important to note that trees do not serve as a suitable representation of a mountain. For individuals residing in apartments, high-rise buildings, townhouses, condominiums, or rented spaces where outdoor water features are not feasible, placing an indoor water feature in the recommended area is a suitable alternative. To activate the mountain element in the designated area, tall cupboards or wardrobes, heavy bookcases, or stone statues can be used effectively to stimulate the energy.

Regarding the rear of the property or backyard, if you require a water feature, a pond, or swimming pool, it is recommended in the South (right-hand corner). While this placement is not ideal, it does not bring harm to the household. However, placing the pool in the Southeast (centre) may lead to sickness, and placing it in the East (left-hand corner) may activate lawsuits and result in significant family disharmony.

PERIOD 9

North 1 (337.6° to 352.5°)

External outdoor activation

Install Water and Mountain at the back.

The North 1 property boasts the auspicious Double 9 Stars at the back. North-facing properties are associated with success, charismatic individuals, and abundant wealth. To maximise the positive influences of this chart, it is crucial to incorporate a water feature and a 'mountain' in the backyard. The mountain element can be created using higher ground, landscape mounds, boulders, or a combination of these elements, being at least 3 feet in height. Cleverly designed tiered landscaping or stacked terraces can also be effective in achieving the desired effect. For the water feature, options include a water feature, a pond, or swimming pool, waterfall/a pond, Koi Pond, lake, or spa, placed at the back of the property. If you reside in an apartment, high-rise building, townhouse, condominium, or a rented space where outdoor water features are not feasible, consider placing an indoor water feature in the recommended area. To activate the mountain element in the designated area, you can utilise tall cupboards or wardrobes, heavy bookcases, or stone statues, as these items effectively stimulate the energy.

Regarding your rear or backyard water feature, a pond, or swimming pool, if you desire to have one, it is recommended to locate it in the South. Alternatively, the pool can touch the Southeast if there are individuals in the household who are teachers, writers, or have a public persona. However, it is important to avoid placing water features in the Southeast as they may lead to affairs. Moreover, placing water in the Southwest (right-hand corner) can activate sickness, diseases, and persistent health issues.

PERIOD 9

North 2 (352.6° to 7.5°)

North 3 (7.6° to 22.5)

External outdoor activation

Mountain and Water required in the front.

The North 2 or 3 facing property features the auspicious Double 9 Stars in the front. North-facing properties are associated with success, charismatic individuals, and good fortune in wealth accumulation. Additionally, such properties bring opportunities for business success and fruitful business relationships that may extend globally. To fully harness the positive energy and promote health, prosperity, and harmony, it is recommended to incorporate significant water and a 'mountain' element in the front of the house. For those living in apartments, high-rise buildings, townhouses, condominiums, or rented spaces where outdoor water features are not feasible, placing a water feature indoors in the recommended area can still activate the desired energy. To activate the mountain element in the recommended area, items such as tall cupboard or wardrobes, heavy bookcases, or stone statues can be utilised effectively.

The rear or backyard does not require a water feature, a pond, or swimming pool, but if you desire to have one, you have the flexibility to choose its location within the backyard. However, the South and Southwest sectors, particularly the centre and right-hand corner, are considered the most favourable for pool placement.

PERIOD 9

Northeast 1

External outdoor activation

Water and Mountain required at the back.

The Northeast 1 property has the presence of the double two 9 stars at the back. These properties are associated with prosperity and nobility, offering great potential for success. To enhance the positive energy and promote well-being, harmonious relationships, and financial abundance, it is crucial to incorporate both a water feature and a 'mountain' element in the back garden. The 'mountain' can take the form of higher ground, landscape mounds, boulders, or a combination of these elements, with a minimum height of 3 feet. Creative options such as tiered landscaping or stacked terraces can also be utilised effectively. Placing a water feature at the back, such as a water feature, a pond, or swimming pool, waterfall/pond, Koi Pond, lake, or spa, will further activate the positive energy. For individuals residing in apartments, high-rise buildings, townhouses, condominiums, or rented spaces where outdoor water features are not feasible, placing a water feature indoors in the recommended area can still harness the desired energy. To activate the 'mountain' element in the designated area, utilising tall cupboard or wardrobes, heavy bookcases, or stone statues will effectively enhance the energy flow.

When considering the rear or backyard of your property, a water feature, a pond, or swimming pool, if you desire to have one, is advised to be in the Southwest sector. It is acceptable if a portion of the pool design extends into the South sector without causing harm. However, it is important to avoid placing water features in the West (right-hand corner) as it may potentially activate unfavourable circumstances.

PERIOD 9

Northeast 2 (37.6° to 52.5°)

Northeast 3 (52.6° to 67.5°)

External outdoor activation

Mountain and Water required in the front.

This Northeast 2 and 3 remarkable chart showcases the powerful double 9 stars in the front. The Northeast-facing properties signify prosperity and nobility. To fully harness the potential of this chart, it is essential to incorporate both water and a mountain element in the front of the property. For the water element, consider installing a substantial stone fountain, a pond, or waterfall. As for the mountain, it can be created using higher ground, landscape mounds, boulders, or a combination of these features. Ensure that the mountain is at least 3 feet or higher. If you reside in an apartment, high-rise building, townhouse, condominium, or rented space where outdoor water features are not feasible, you can place a water feature indoors in the recommended area to activate the desired energy. To activate the mountain element in the designated area, utilise tall cupboards or wardrobes, heavy bookcases, or stone statues, as they will effectively stimulate the energy flow.

Your rear or backyard doesn't require a water feature, a pond, or swimming pool, but if you desire to have one, it can be located anywhere in the backyard. However, for optimal luck, consider placing in the South or West corners. It is important to note that when positioning the water in the South, ensure it is not between 176.6° to 187.5°, as this may activate affairs and potentially disrupt harmony.

PERIOD 9

East 1 (67.6° to 82.5°)

External outdoor activation

Install Water and Mountain at the Back.

The East 1 exceptional property boasts the presence of the double 9 stars at the back. These properties have the potential to nurture residents with remarkable academic achievements or immense success in the field of education. To harness the full power of this chart, it is crucial to incorporate a water feature and a 'mountain' element in the back garden. The 'mountain' can be created using higher ground, landscape mounds, boulders, or a combination of these features, ensuring that it stands at least 3 feet or higher. Alternatively, intelligently designed tiered landscaping or a series of stacked terraces can also be effective. For the water feature, consider installing a water feature, a pond, or swimming pool, waterfall, a pond, Koi Pond, lake, or hot tub/spa in the back garden. However, if you live in an apartment, high-rise building, townhouse, condominium, or rented space where outdoor water features are not feasible, you can place a water feature indoors in the recommended area. To activate the mountain element in the designated area, you can use tall cupboard or wardrobes, heavy bookcases, or stone statues. These elements will effectively stimulate the flow of energy and enhance the desired effects.

As you require a water feature, a pond, or swimming pool, in the rear or back, the ideal locations are the West (centre) or the Northwest. It is worth noting that pool designs often touch two sectors, so you can maximise benefits and energetic impact by combining them.

PERIOD 9

East 2 (82.6° to 97.5°)

East 3 (97.6° to 112.5°)

External outdoor activation

Mountain and Water required in the front.

The East 2 and 3 auspicious chart reveals the presence of two 9 stars in the front. The properties facing East have the potential to cultivate righteous, charismatic, loyal, and faithful professionals such as doctors, lawyers, and philosophers who can attain both wealth and nobility. To unlock the full potential of this chart, it is essential to incorporate both water and a mountain element in the front of the property. For the water element, consider installing a substantial stone fountain, a pond, or waterfall. These features not only add beauty but also enhance the energetic flow. The mountain element can be created using higher ground, landscape mounds, or boulders, or a combination of these elements. It is recommended that the mountain stands at least 3 feet or higher. If you live in an apartment, high-rise building, townhouse, condominium, or rented space where outdoor water features are not feasible, you can place a water feature indoors in the designated area. To activate the mountain energy indoors, utilise tall cupboards or wardrobes, heavy bookcases, or stone statues in the recommended area.

Regarding a backyard water feature, a pond, or swimming pool, if you desire to have one, the Southwest is the optimal location for the best results. A water feature, a pond, or swimming pool in this area can enhance the auspicious energy. However, it is important to note that water in the West (centre) may activate various types of disasters, so it is advisable to avoid placing water features or pool in that specific area.

PERIOD 9

Southeast 1 (112.6° to 127.5°)

External outdoor activation

Mountain and Water required in the front.

The auspicious Southeast 1 chart showcases the presence of two 9 stars in the front. The properties facing Southeast have the potential to nurture exceptional talent in sports, including martial arts. Moreover, the occupants of this house, especially the children, may excel in scientific fields that require technical expertise. To fully activate the positive energy of this chart, it is important to incorporate both water and a mountain element in the front of the property. To introduce the water element, consider installing a substantial stone fountain, a pond, or waterfall. These water features not only add visual appeal but also enhance the energetic flow. As for the mountain element, it can be created using higher ground, landscape mounds, boulders, or a combination of these elements. It is recommended that the mountain stands at least 3 feet or higher. In cases where outdoor water features are not feasible due to living in an apartment, high-rise building, townhouse, condominium, or rented space, you can place a water feature indoors in the recommended area. To activate the mountain energy indoors, utilise a tall cupboard or wardrobes, heavy bookcases, or stone statues strategically placed in the designated area.

The rear or backyard does not require a water feature, a pond, or swimming pool, but if you desire to have one, the West (left-hand corner) is a suitable location, although it is not considered ideal. While it will not harm the occupants, it is

important to avoid having water in the West between 262.6° to 277.5° as it may potentially lead to affairs. By adhering to these guidelines, you can optimise the positive energy flow in your home.

PERIOD 9

Southeast 2 (127.6° to 142.5°)

Southeast 3 (142.6° to 157.5°)

External outdoor activation

Water and Mountain required at the back.

The Southeast 2 and 3 property is very special in Period 9 exhibiting the double 9 stars at the back. Each sector also has combination of ten with mountain star and natal star combining to 10. This chart has the potential to nurture individuals with high moral values, nobility, trustworthiness. A Southeast-facing property is particularly suited for philosophers, performers, singers, and artists. To fully harness the positive energy of this chart, it is essential to incorporate both a water feature and a 'mountain' element in the back garden. The 'mountain' element can be created using higher ground, landscape mounds, or boulders. Alternatively, a combination of these elements can be used, with the mountain being at least 3 foot or higher. Additionally, smartly designed tiered landscaping or a series of stacked terraces can be employed to enhance the visual appeal and energetic flow of the space. To introduce the water element, consider installing a water feature, a pond, or swimming pool, waterfall/pond, Koi Pond, lake, or spa at the back of the property. These water features not only contribute to a serene ambiance but also activate the positive energy. For individuals residing in apartments, high-rise buildings, townhouses, condominiums, or rented spaces where outdoor water features are not feasible, it is recommended to place a water feature indoors in the recommended area. To activate the mountain energy indoors, utilise a tall cupboards or wardrobes, heavy bookcases, or stone statues strategically placed in the designated area. These elements effectively stimulate the desired energy flow within the space.

Your rear or backyard requires a water feature, a pond, or swimming pool, the ideal locations would be the Northwest (centre) or the West (left-hand corner). Pool designs often touch two sectors, allowing for flexibility in placement. By adhering to these recommendations, you can optimise the positive energy flow and create an auspicious environment on your property.

HOW TO OPTIMISE YOUR PERIOD 8 BUILT PROPERTY

PERIOD 8

South 1 (157.6° to 172.5°)

What changes can you make for your Period 8 South 1 facing property for Period 9?

To make the most of your property in Period 9, consider incorporating a mountain-like feature in the southern part of your property. This can take the form of elevated terrain, landscaped mounds, walls around a courtyard, large rocks, or even a combination of these elements. Additionally, it is recommended to introduce a water feature, such as a fountain, in the southwestern area of your front yard.

PERIOD 8

South 2 (172.6° to 187.5°)

South 3 (187.6° to 202.5°)

What changes can you make for your Period 8 South 2 or 3 facing property for Period 9?

Make the most of your property by incorporating a mountain-like feature within the southern part of your property. This "mountain" can take various forms, such as higher ground, landscaped mounds, walls enclosing a courtyard, sizeable rocks, or even a combination of these elements. Furthermore, it is highly recommended to introduce a water feature, such as a fountain, in the southwestern area of your front yard.

PERIOD 8

Southwest 1 (202.6° to 217.5°)

What changes can you make for your Period 8 Southwest 1 facing property for Period 9?

Embrace Period 9 luck by incorporating a mountain-like feature in the western section of your front yard. This "mountain" can take various forms, such as elevated terrain, landscaped mounds, substantial rocks, or even a combination of these elements. Additionally, it is highly recommended to introduce a water feature in the northern area of your backyard, such as a fountain, a pond, or pool. However, it's important to avoid placing the water feature between 352.6 degrees to 7.5 degrees in the northern direction, as this location may inadvertently activate affairs.

PERIOD 8

Southwest 2 (217.6° to 232.5°)

Southwest 3 (232.6° to 247.5°)

What changes can you make for your Period 8 Southwest 2 or 3 facing property for Period 9?

Make the most of Period 9 luck in your property with incorporating a mountain-like feature in the eastern part of your property. This "mountain" can take various forms, such as elevated terrain, landscaped mounds, raised brick decking, substantial rocks, or even a combination of these elements. Additionally, it is highly recommended to introduce a water feature in the southern area of your front yard, such as a fountain. This addition can bring an additional touch of tranquillity and beauty to your outdoor space.

PERIOD 8

West 1 (247.6° to 262.5°)

What changes can you make for your Period 8 West 1 facing property for Period 9?

Consider incorporating a mountain-like feature in the southwest section of your front backyard. This "mountain" can take various forms, such as elevated terrain, landscaped mounds, walls enclosing a courtyard, substantial rocks, or even a combination of these elements. Furthermore, it is highly recommended to introduce a water feature in the southeastern area of your backyard, such as a pond, pool, or fountain. Adding this water feature can create a serene and captivating ambiance in your outdoor space.

PERIOD 8

West 2 (262.6° to 277.5°)

West 3 (277.6° to 292.5°)

What changes can you make for your Period 8 West 2 or 3 facing property for Period 9?

Make the most of your property luck by incorporating a mountain-like feature in the northeast corner of your backyard. This "mountain" can take various forms, such as elevated terrain, landscaped mounds, substantial rocks, or even a combination of these elements. Additionally, it is highly recommended to introduce a water feature in the northwest area of your front yard, such as a fountain. This addition can bring a refreshing and aesthetically pleasing touch to your outdoor space.

PERIOD 8

Northwest 1 (292.6° to 307.5°)

What changes can you make for your Period 8 Northwest 1 facing property for Period 9?

Consider incorporating a mountain-like feature in the western area of your front yard. This "mountain" can take various forms, such as elevated terrain, landscaped mounds, walls enclosing a courtyard, substantial rocks, or even a combination of these elements. However, it is important to note that the 9 facing star is trapped in the middle and cannot be activated with water. Nevertheless, if you activate

the 8 facing star as recommended, you will enhance prosperity for your home. So, by following this recommendation, you can maximise the positive energy and abundance in your living space.

PERIOD 8

Northwest 2 (307.6° to 322.5°)

Northwest 3 (322.6° to 337.5°)

What changes can you make for your Period 8 Northwest 2 or 3 facing property for Period 9?

Make the most of your property by incorporating a mountain-like feature in the eastern corner of your backyard. This "mountain" can take various forms, such as elevated terrain, landscaped mounds, raised brick decking, substantial rocks, or even a combination of these elements. However, it is important to note that the 9 facing star is trapped in the middle and cannot be activated with water. Nevertheless, if you activate the 8 facing star as recommended, you will enhance prosperity for your home. By following this suggestion, you can cultivate an atmosphere of abundance and success within your living space.

PERIOD 8

North 1 (337.6° to 352.5°)

What changes can you make for your Period 8 North 1 facing property for Period 9?

For Period 9 incorporate a mountain-like feature in the southwest corner of your backyard. This "mountain" can take various forms, such as elevated terrain, landscaped mounds, raised brick decking, substantial rocks, or even a combination of these elements. Additionally, it is recommended to install a water feature in the south area, particularly where the 9 facing star is located. This water feature can be a pool, a pond, or fountain, bringing a sense of tranquillity and beauty to your outdoor space while enhancing the positive energy associated with the 9 facing star. By incorporating these elements, you can create an inviting and harmonious environment for your home.

PERIOD 8

North 2 (352.6° to 7.5°)

North 3 (7.6° to 22.5)

What changes can you make for your Period 8 North 2 or 3 facing property for Period 9?

To make the most of your property luck incorporate a mountain-like feature in the northeast area of your front yard. This "mountain" can take various forms, such as elevated terrain, landscaped mounds, walls enclosing a courtyard, substantial rocks, or even a combination of these elements. Additionally, it is highly recommended to place a water feature in the north area of your front yard, such as a fountain. It's important to note that this is the only Period 8 chart where the 9 facing star is in the front, which is considered very auspicious. By implementing these elements, you can enhance the positive energy and harmony of your living space, inviting good fortune and prosperity into your home.

PERIOD 8

Northeast 1 (22.6° to 37.5°)

What changes can you make for your Period 8 Northeast 1 facing property for Period 9?

Make the most of Period 9 by incorporating a mountain-like feature in the northern area of your front yard. This "mountain" can take various forms, such as elevated terrain, landscaped mounds, walls enclosing a courtyard, substantial rocks, or even a combination of these elements. Furthermore, it is highly recommended to place a water feature in the western area of your backyard, such as a pond, pool, or fountain. This addition can create a sense of serenity and beauty in your outdoor space, allowing you to enjoy the soothing presence of water. By implementing these elements, you can enhance the positive energy and harmonious atmosphere of your home, attracting abundance and prosperity into your life.

PERIOD 8

Northeast 2 (37.6° to 52.5°)

Northeast 3 (52.6° to 67.5°)

What changes can you make for your Period 8 Northeast 2 or 3 facing property for Period 9?

It is recommended you incorporate a mountain-like feature in the southern corner of your backyard. This "mountain" can take various forms, such as elevated terrain, landscaped mounds, raised brick or stone decking, substantial rocks, or even a combination of these elements. Additionally, it is highly recommended to place a water feature in the eastern area of your front yard, such as a fountain. This addition can bring a touch of elegance and tranquillity to your outdoor space. By implementing these elements, you can create a harmonious and inviting atmosphere in your home, amplifying the positive energy, and fostering a sense of abundance and prosperity.

PERIOD 8

East 1 (67.6° to 82.5°)

What changes can you make for your Period 8 East 1 facing property for Period 9?

Tap into your property luck by incorporating a mountain-like feature in the southeast area of your front yard. This "mountain" can take various forms, such as elevated terrain, landscaped mounds, walls enclosing a courtyard, substantial rocks, or even a combination of these elements. Additionally, it is highly recommended to place a water feature in the southwest area of your backyard, such as a fountain, a pond, or pool. By incorporating these elements, you can create a visually stunning and serene environment in your outdoor space, fostering a sense of tranquillity and relaxation. These enhancements can bring positive energy and harmony into your home, allowing you to enjoy a soothing and inviting atmosphere.

PERIOD 8

East 2 (82.6° to 97.5°)

East 3 (97.6° to 112.5°)

What changes can you make for your Period 8 East 2 and 3 facing property for Period 9?

Make the most of your property by incorporating a mountain-like feature in the northwest corner of your backyard. This "mountain" can take various forms, such as elevated terrain, landscaped mounds, raised brick or stone decking, substantial rocks, or even a combination of these elements. Additionally, it is highly recommended to place a water feature in the northeast area of your front yard, such as a fountain. This addition can bring a sense of elegance and serenity to your outdoor space, creating a soothing ambiance. By implementing these elements, you can enhance the positive energy and harmonious atmosphere of your home, fostering a welcoming and prosperous environment for you and your loved ones.

PERIOD 8

Southeast 1 (112.6° to 127.5°)

What changes can you make for your Period 8 Southeast 1 facing property for Period 9?

To take advantage of Period 9 energy it is recommended to install a pond, pool, or fountain in the western corner of your backyard. However, it's important to note that the water feature should not be positioned between 262.6 degrees to 277.5 degrees, as it may activate unwanted affairs. It's crucial to maintain a harmonious energy flow in your home. Additionally, it's worth mentioning that the 9-mountain star is trapped in the middle and cannot be represented. However, by activating the 8 mountain, you can bring forth a sense of nobility and prosperity to your living space. By incorporating these elements, you can create a serene and prosperous environment that promotes positive energy and enhances the overall ambiance of your home.

PERIOD 8

Southeast 2 (127.6° to 142.5°)

Southeast 3 (142.6° to 157.5°)

What changes can you make for your Period 8 Southeast 2 or 3 facing property for Period 9?

For Period 9, if you don't already have a water feature in the southeast area of your property, it is highly recommended to install a fountain in the eastern area of your front yard. This addition can bring a sense of beauty and tranquillity to your outdoor space. It's important to note that the 9-mountain star is trapped in the middle and cannot be represented. However, by activating the 8 mountain, you can invite a sense of nobility and prosperity into your home. By incorporating these elements and adjustments, you can create a harmonious and auspicious environment that promotes positive energy flow and enhances the overall ambiance of your living space.

FLYING STAR CHARTERISTICS AND MEANING

FLYING STAR 1

Flying Star 1 is associated with positive attributes and growing energy such as knowledge, wisdom, a good reputation, status, authority, and recognition of one's efforts. A nobleman star full of future prosperity. When the Flying Star 1 appears as a Facing Star, it indicates that wealth and financial pursuits will benefit. As a Sitting Star, it brings good prospects for relationships and networking.

Flying Star 1 is linked to Kan Gua and the Water element, as seen in the Luo Shu and Eight Trigrams (Ba gua). In its negative mode, the Flying Star 1 can lead to ignorance, depression, misery, lack of intelligence, and in severe cases, incidents that cause loss. It can also signify the possibility of losing items and expulsion, influenced by the negative attributes of the Water element.

FLYING STAR 2

Flying Star 2 has generally been considered negative, particularly during Period 8, but in Period 9 during its positive form, Flying Star 2 brings good health, excellent recuperative capabilities, and high productivity. Its association with the Earth element augurs well for wealth and property-related pursuits in Periods 9 and 1.

Representing the Earth element and Kun Gua (Southwest). In Period 8 the Flying Star 2 was associated with illness, health-related problems (physical and mental), and contagion during Period 8.

FLYING STAR 3

Flying Star 3 is generally regarded as negative, particularly during Periods 8 and 9. It represents the Wood element and Zhen Gua (East) and is associated with misunderstandings, arguments, disputes, legal entanglements, robbery, and theft. Sectors occupied by the Flying Star 3, especially in an Annual Flying Stars chart for a specific year, should be avoided, particularly for those who frequently need to socialise or network. Paradoxically, the Flying Star 3 is an action and movement star and allows for excellent communication and leadership opportunities in its positive form. It supports anyone striving to bounce back from defeat or failure, facilitating their path to success.

FLYING STAR 4

Flying Star 4 is generally considered a neutral star but is also known as the Academic or Scholastic Star. It supports endeavours related to seeking knowledge, making it suitable for studying, academic pursuits, scholarly activities, and the accumulation of knowledge. Representing the Wood element and Xun Gua (Southeast), Flying Star 4 should be used with caution as it can bring about relationship problems, scandals, and adultery in its negative mode. Negative Forms that affect the property can exacerbate such undesirable situations.

FLYING STAR 5

Flying Star 5 is the most dangerous and negative of all the Nine Stars, especially as a Facing Star or Sitting Star. It signifies serious setbacks, repercussions, bankruptcy, catastrophes, disasters, and diseases. As a novice, it is safe to consider Flying Star 5 as a negative star about 95% of the time. Activities that disturb, renovate, or use a sector occupied by Flying Star 5 only activate its harmful energies. Advanced practitioners may consider Flying Star 5 as a Wealth Star under specific circumstances when used appropriately. But for the novice for now, understand that the Flying Star 5 can bring about great accomplishments, capabilities, and good wealth prospects if its positive energies are successfully harnessed. But as Fire gives life to earth the negative attributes of Flying Star 5 will mainly be felt during Period 9.

FLYING STAR 6

Flying Star 6 is generally regarded as a positive star, symbolising authority, power, influence, nobility, respect, and career advancement prospects. However, it can have a flip side, resulting in loneliness, egoistic and dogmatic behaviour, broken relationships, and family issues. Flying Star 6 represents the Metal Element and Qian Gua (Northwest). Metal can heat up and cool down quickly, which can be applied metaphorically to relationships, where the "loving feeling" can fade quickly.

FLYING STAR 7

Flying Star 7 is generally an undesirable star, representing Dui Gua (West). It brings about theft, robbery, slanderous remarks, hazards caused by fire and sharp objects, and other undesirable situations. However, in its positive form, Flying Star 7 is beneficial for metaphysical and spiritual pursuits, communication, and relationships. Marketing, advertising, salespeople, or those interested in metaphysics may tap into its energies in its positive form.

FLYING STAR 8

Flying Star 8 energies in Period 9 are retreating as it is now a retired star of little power but still positive and usable about 90% of the time, making it a stable Wealth Star. Representing Gen Gua (Northeast). During Period 8, having Flying Star 8 in a Flying Stars Chart was advantageous. When a Flying Star 8 Facing Star is utilised for income, wealth, or asset-related pursuits, it can bring stable results, provided diligent effort is put into those endeavours. However, it poses health and safety hazards to young children and individuals who neglect their limbs, backbone, and spinal cord. In a household, its negative presence can lead to introverted and reclusive behaviour.

FLYING STAR 9

The Prosperous and prominent Flying Star 9 is incredibly auspicious, representing Li Gua (South). Flying Star 9 brings forth a multitude of positive attributes and blessings. Its presence signifies a time of great fortune and abundance, showering those in its influence with a cascade of favourable energies and opportunities.

First and foremost, Flying Star 9 embodies beauty and elegance. It bestows an air of grace and refinement upon its surroundings, making it the perfect star to enhance the aesthetic appeal of any space. Whether it's through art, design, or simply creating a harmonious atmosphere, Flying Star 9 inspires a sense of visual delight and appreciation.

In addition to its enchanting beauty, the Flying Star 9 heralds joyful moments and celebrations. It invites an atmosphere of happiness and merriment, making it an ideal star for festive occasions and special gatherings. Its presence evokes a sense of pure delight and encourages the creation of cherished memories that will be treasured for years to come.

Beyond its ability to bring joy, the Flying Star 9 holds the power to manifest promotions and recognition in one's career. It serves as a catalyst for success, opening doors to new opportunities and propelling individuals forward in their professional endeavours. With its positive influence, Flying Star 9 paves the way for career advancement and the acknowledgment of one's hard work and accomplishments.

Flying Star 9 is deeply associated with prosperity and abundance. Its energies attract financial growth, wealth accumulation, and overall prosperity in various aspects of life. With this star's blessings, individuals can experience a significant increase in their material well-being and enjoy a life of abundance and financial security.

Not only does Flying Star 9 bring external rewards, but it also nurtures positive relationships and social connections. It fosters harmonious interactions and facilitates the formation of meaningful bonds with influential individuals. Whether in personal or professional settings, Flying Star 9 acts as a bridge, connecting people and fostering a supportive network that can contribute to personal and collective success.

Furthermore, Flying Star 9 ignites hope and a flame of personal growth and self-improvement. It encourages individuals to embrace their potential, develop their talents, and strive for excellence. With its positive influence, Flying Star 9 empowers individuals to overcome obstacles and achieve their goals, enabling personal and professional fulfillment.

Flying Star 9 brings blessings to relationships, promoting harmony, love, and understanding. It strengthens family bonds, deepens friendships, and supports the blossoming of romantic partnerships. Under the auspices of Flying Star 9, relationships thrive, creating a nurturing and supportive environment for all involved.

Flying Star 9 in Period 9 is a beacon of positivity and abundance. With its blessings, it brings forth beauty, joy, prosperity, success, harmonious relationships, personal growth, and so much more. Embracing the energy of the Flying Star 9 can lead to a life filled with abundance, happiness, and fulfillment.

But while Flying Star 9 in Period 9 is predominantly associated with positive attributes, it's important to acknowledge the potential negative aspects that can arise under its influence. Despite its auspicious nature, Flying Star 9 can bring about scandals, litigation problems, fire hazards, and even psychological challenges such as paranoia and addiction. It is crucial to maintain a balanced approach and mitigate any potential negative effects by practicing caution, maintaining vigilance, and implementing appropriate preventive measures to safeguard against these undesirable outcomes.

When it comes to Flying Stars, the Prosperous Flying Star 9 is considered positive, especially in Period 9 starting from February 4, 2024. To tap into its beneficial energies, it is ideal to have the (Main) Door, a Yang feature, located in the sector that contains the number 9 Facing Star. Additionally, external water formations can also activate the number 9 Facing Star.

Furthermore, aim to support the number 9 Sitting Star with Yin features such as a bedroom or a mountain located outside the sector with the number 9 Sitting Star. This enhances its effects and positively impacts the health and relationships of the occupants in that sector of the home.

ACTIVATING AND DEACTIVATING FLYING STARS

In Feng Shui, it is crucial to maintain a balance between Yang and Yin Chi. Therefore, if Facing Stars can be activated by Yang features like water, they can also be deactivated by Yin features like mountains. Similarly, Sitting Stars activated by Yin features like mountains can be deactivated by Yang features like water.

For instance, if a mountain is present outside a number 9 Facing Star, it deactivates the wealth-generating effects of this Star. Similarly, a Sitting Star with a lake outside its sector will be deactivated and unable to exert its beneficial energies.

It is important to note that this principle applies mainly to negative Stars. Negative Facing and Sitting Stars can be deactivated or neutralised using the concept of Forms/Situations superseding Formulas. For example, an inauspicious Facing Star can be deactivated by the presence of a mountain or through inactivity, stillness, and quietness.

81 FLYING STAR COMBINATION MEANING

1-1

The 1-1 flying star combination brings positive outcomes related to intelligence, wealth, wisdom, travel, recognition, academic success, and romance. It favours academic pursuits and can lead to a good reputation and widespread recognition, particularly for young men. However, there are negative aspects such as potential issues with alcoholism, infidelity, legal matters, and health problems. Nonetheless, it remains highly beneficial for academic endeavours and individuals with Gua 3 or 4, as water nourishes wood, associated with these Gua numbers.

1-2

The 1-2 flying star combination has significant implications. It indicates public support and the potential for a high position, particularly for women in government, healthcare, or corporations. However, it brings unfavourable outcomes for middle-aged men, including humiliation and dominance by their wives. It signifies a lack of support, disputes, and the possibility of divorce. This combination may lead to health issues such as abdominal problems, swelling, bleeding, and an unattractive appearance. Men may experience infidelity and digestive problems, while women may face stomach and gynaecological issues. It also suggests disharmony within the household due to controlling wives.

1-3

The 1-3 flying star combination signifies wealth, fame, popularity, and thriving new industries or businesses. It brings luck to families with many children and promotes the eldest son's success and recognition. This combination also suggests the possibility of a new baby and increased travel opportunities. However, there are potential negative aspects such as accidents, obstacles, lawsuits, robberies, and bankruptcy. It may lead to arguments, disputes, and deception within the family. Individuals influenced by this combination may have heightened temperaments. Overall, the 1-3 combination brings potential for travel and positive news in that regard.

1-4

The 1-4 flying star combination is highly beneficial for scholarly achievements, media attention, and academic pursuits. It supports irrigation systems and the mining industry. Individuals influenced by this combination are likely to receive recognition and publicity. It is advantageous for investments in precious metals and has Peach Blossom energy for romantic relationships. However, excessive water energy can lead to scandals, misbehaviour, and criminal activities. It may enhance sexual appeal but could result in promiscuity and forgery. Unfavourable positions or excessive water can lead to affairs and negative romances. Relationship issues may arise with nearby sharp structures, while a peaceful and green environment fosters academic success.

1-5

The 1-5 flying star combination indicates a favourable influence for scholars and achieving success in exams. It supports intellectual pursuits and the cultivation of wise children. The 5 star holds significant power during its own Period, bringing wealth and influence. However, when out of timing, it can bring troubles and disasters. This combination also carries potential risks related to water, such as bankruptcy and water retention. Health issues associated with this combination include hearing problems, kidney issues, and various genital diseases. The negative aspects of the flying star 5, such as cancer, poisoning, and miscarriages, are emphasised. Additionally, this combination is associated with genital diseases.

1-6

The 1-6 flying star combination signifies intelligence and financial skills. It supports artistic and literary pursuits, teaching, and scholarly careers. It can lead to high rank in fields like the military or law enforcement. Happy occasions such as marriages are associated with these stars. However, potential health issues include migraines and mental disorders. Conflicts between fathers and sons and criminal activities may arise. Caution is advised with sharp objects to prevent accidents. This combination is advantageous for the armed forces, police, and sports. Negative forms outside this area may indicate a risk of head injuries.

1-7

The 1-7 flying star combination signifies conflict and potential legal issues. It indicates arguments, disputes, and the possibility of lawsuits. Strained relationships and opposition from family members may occur. Temperamental outbursts and lack of harmony are also likely. Caution is advised in love affairs to avoid being deceived. Attacks from animals, including pets, are possible. Health issues may include heart problems and various disorders. Resolving conflicts is crucial for maintaining peace and harmony in relationships and the household.

1-8

The 1-8 flying star combination brings auspicious energy related to success, prosperity, and travel. It indicates the potential for wealth, fame, and recognition in various endeavours. This combination is particularly favourable for business and career advancements, leading to promotions, financial gains, and positive opportunities. The energy of these stars provides protection and support, attracting favourable circumstances and blessings. This combination may cause hearing problems, especially in the elderly and very young. Additionally, painful illnesses such as kidney stones can crop up from time to time. Overall, it is a fortunate combination that can bring good news, favourable outcomes, and an overall positive influence on one's life.

1-9

The 1-9 flying star combination brings auspicious energy that signifies growth, expansion, and success in various aspects of life. It indicates favourable conditions for achieving wealth, prosperity, abundance, and high social status. This

combination is particularly beneficial for career advancements, business ventures, and financial gains. It supports the development of leadership skills and attracts positive opportunities for growth. The energy of these stars promotes good fortune and favourable outcomes. It also signifies the potential for long-distance travel and exploration. However, it is important to note that promiscuous individuals should exercise caution when affected by this combination, as there is a higher risk of venereal and sexually transmitted diseases. Miscarriages may occur when this combination is unfortunate, and cardiac problems may be more prevalent.

2-1

The 2-1 flying star combination signifies harmonious and auspicious energy with positive influences on various aspects of life. It supports intelligence, creativity, and academic success, making it beneficial for students and scholars. Financial prosperity and harmonious relationships are also likely. Recognition for talents and abilities is expected. A balanced approach to life is encouraged. However, health issues such as stomach problems and digestive issues may occur for men, while women may face gastric-related problems and upset bowels. Caution is advised regarding abortions for women and a potential decrease in men's sex life.

2-2

The 2-2 flying star combination represents harmonious energy that brings stability and balance to life. It fosters relationship harmony, love, and companionship. It creates a peaceful home environment and nurtures caregiving qualities. This combination instils a sense of security and emotional well-being. However, it can lead to greed and health issues, including abdominal cramps for women. It signifies a matriarchal influence and authority within the family. Unfavourable cycles in Periods 3 to 8 may bring severe illness and despair.

2-3

The 2-3 flying star combination represents dynamic and transformative energy with influences on various aspects of life. It signifies growth, progress, and expansion in career and business. This combination brings opportunities for advancement and success, but it can also bring trouble such as disputes, lawsuits, and family breakups. Older ladies may be particularly affected, experiencing arthritis. Despite challenges, the 2-3 combination promotes adaptability and positive communication. It fosters beneficial relationships and symbolises a period of growth and favourable outcomes.

2-4

The 2-4 flying star combination represents a harmonious and auspicious energy that influences various aspects of life. It signifies stability, growth, and prosperity in both personal academic and professional endeavours. Money can be made via property. However, caution should be exercised as it has been associated with mental illnesses and tensions between mothers and daughters-in-law. It is also advisable to be careful during outdoor activities, as there is a possibility of attacks from dangerous animals. Despite these potential challenges, the 2-4 combination still supports family unity, happiness, and domestic harmony. It brings financial stability and abundance, attracting wealth and material gains. This combination encourages a balanced approach to life, combining practicality with creativity.

2-5

The timely 2-5 combination signifies abundant wealth, growth of a large family, and success for esteemed judges and military personnel. The 5 star holds the power of kingship and wealth during its own Period. However, when untimely, it brings catastrophic outcomes. This deadly combination has severe consequences, including fatal outcomes, illnesses like cancer and appendicitis, and unwanted abortions. It presents obstacles and hinders success, with respiratory issues and immune disorders prevailing. The 2-5 combination fuels conflicts, gossip, and strained relationships. Caution in communication is essential to avoid disputes. Overcoming these challenges requires resilience and proactive measures for health and harmony.

2-6

The 2-6 flying star combination said to represents an affluent and easy life with dynamic and transformative energy that influences various aspects of life. It signifies the potential for growth, progress, and positive changes in career and personal endeavours. This combination is particularly favourable for creative pursuits, innovation, and self-expression. It supports the development of leadership skills and encourages taking initiative. The 2-6 combination also promotes harmonious relationships and teamwork, fostering collaboration and cooperation. It signifies the potential for financial stability and material abundance, especially via property and real estate ventures. But scrooge tendencies maybe developed. Overall, the 2-6 combination symbolises a period of growth, transformation, and favourable outcomes in one's endeavours.

2-7

The 2-7 flying star combination influences partnerships and collaborations, fostering teamwork and successful ventures. However, conflicts and power struggles may arise, leading to disputes and arguments. Open communication is crucial to navigate these challenges. When managed well, this combination brings financial abundance, but wise spending is necessary to prevent loss. The presence of the flying star 9 suggests the possibility of affairs and fire hazards. Mindfulness and proactive measures are essential to maximise the positive aspects and minimise the negative influences of this combination.

2-8

The 2-8 flying star combination represents powerful and auspicious energy, bringing prosperity and abundance in various aspects of life. It is highly favourable for wealth accumulation, investments, and business ventures. This combination supports career success, promotions, and advancements. It attracts financial stability and long-term property investments. It fosters leadership qualities and personal growth, leading to achievements and recognition. However, excessive self-improvement can lead to detachment. Overall, the 2-8 combination signifies a period of prosperity, financial growth, and favourable outcomes.

2-9

The 2-9 flying star combination represents harmonious and auspicious energy, fostering growth and success in intellectual pursuits. It is highly favourable for students, scholars, and those in education. However, caution is needed to avoid romantic entanglements. Potential eye health issues are associated with this combination. Despite these challenges, the 2-9 combination brings opportunities for personal and professional growth, financial stability, and material gains. It encourages a balanced approach to life and positive communication. Overall, it signifies growth and favourable outcomes in education, intellect, and finance, with the need to navigate romance and prioritise eye health.

3-1

The 3-1 flying star combination offers opportunities for personal and professional growth, especially in the legal field. It enhances argumentative skills and persuasive abilities. However, it's important to be cautious of potential challenges, such as conflicts and legal issues. Effective communication and conflict resolution are essential. This combination may also impact liver health and occasionally cause dizziness. Taking proactive measures for liver health and ensuring personal safety is advised. Despite challenges, the 3-1 combination encourages adaptability and resilience. It symbolises a dynamic period with transformative opportunities in legal industries and beyond.

3-2

The 3-2 flying star combination represents dynamic energy and communication. It fosters partnerships and idea exchange. However, it can also bring challenges and conflicts. Verbal disputes and arguments may arise, requiring effective communication and patience for resolution. The combination may affect the mother-son relationship, necessitating open communication and understanding. Health-wise, it can contribute to stomach-related issues, requiring attention to diet and seeking medical advice if needed. Despite challenges, the 3-2 combination offers growth opportunities. By promoting effective communication and maintaining a healthy lifestyle, individuals can navigate challenges and foster positive relationships.

3-3

The 3-3 flying star combination in Feng Shui is associated with a lack of compassion and a tendency towards cold-heartedness. This can result in disputes, fights, and heightened emotional reactions, including hysteria. It is known as the "Quarrelsome Star" or "Argumentative Star" due to its tendency to create conflicts and disagreements. The presence of this combination brings a hostile atmosphere, increased tension, and a lack of harmony. It is crucial to address and counteract the negative effects of this star to foster a more peaceful and harmonious environment.

3-4

The 3-4 flying star combination represents dynamic and transformative energy. It affects mental and emotional well-being, necessitating self-care and stress management. For males, it enhances attractiveness but requires caution in relationships. Overall, the 3-4 combination signifies dynamic change and calls for emotional awareness and personal growth. By prioritising well-being, individuals navigate challenges and embrace transformation.

3-5

The 3-5 flying star combination presents challenges and risks in various aspects of life. It indicates potential financial loss and instability, health issues related to the liver and infectious diseases, and a higher risk of accidents resulting in broken limbs. Prudence in financial management, caution in daily activities, and proactive

health measures are crucial to mitigate these risks. The 3-5 combination emphasises responsible decision-making, financial discipline, and maintaining good health practices for greater stability and well-being.

3-6

The 3-6 flying star combination has diverse effects on individuals and their surroundings. It brings government and business support, success, and political luck. However, headaches are a common occurrence with this combination, requiring attention and management. Accidental injuries, especially with sharp metal objects, are also a concern. Caution and awareness of surroundings are essential to minimise risks. Family relationships may be affected, necessitating patience and understanding to navigate conflicts. Prioritising physical well-being, managing headaches, and ensuring safety are crucial. By being proactive and mindful, individuals can overcome challenges and strive for a harmonious life.

3-7

The 3-7 flying star combination presents challenging energy with negative influences on various aspects of life. It is associated with conflicts, disputes, and disagreements, leading to strained relationships and potential legal disputes. Financial challenges and instability may arise as well. Caution, peaceful resolutions, and careful financial planning are necessary to mitigate these effects. Proactive management of conflicts and responsible financial practices can help individuals strive for harmony and stability in their lives despite the challenges posed by the 3-7 combination.

3-8

The 3-8 flying star combination presents challenging and potentially negative energy that impacts various aspects of life. It is associated with health issues like miscarriages, heart disease, and asthma. Family discord and potential disintegration can arise from this combination, leading to tensions and conflicts. It may also have an influence on sexual orientation. Open communication, understanding, and reconciliation are crucial in mitigating the negative effects on family dynamics. Sensitivity, respect, and acceptance are important when discussing sexual orientation. Overall, addressing health concerns, nurturing family relationships, and embracing diversity are key to navigating the challenges of the 3-8 combination and striving for overall well-being.

3-9

The 3-9 flying star combination represents a dynamic and influential energy that can have both positive and negative impacts on various aspects of life. It supports intellectual pursuits, creativity, and problem-solving capabilities. However, it may bring potential fire-related risks and challenges. Exercise caution and take safety precautions to prevent accidents. This combination also signifies opportunities for career growth and success. By harnessing intelligence and being mindful of fire-related risks, individuals can navigate the 3-9 combination and strive for personal and professional growth.

4-1

The 4-1 flying star combination represents a powerful and auspicious energy that influences various aspects of life. It enhances excellence in academia and studying, showcasing exceptional academic abilities and a thirst for knowledge. This combination also supports a strong reputation in writing and research, leading to recognition and respect in fields such as literature, journalism, and scientific research. Additionally, it encourages spiritual pursuits, fostering inner connection and growth. For women, the 4-1 combination brings romantic opportunities and enhances attractiveness. Overall, the 4-1 combination signifies a harmonious blend of intellectual pursuits, spiritual growth, and romantic possibilities, leading to personal and professional fulfillment.

4-2

The 4-2 flying star combination represents a transformative energy that influences various aspects of life. It encourages studies in metaphysics, culture, and esoteric knowledge, fostering deep understanding. However, conflicts between mothers and daughters-in-law may arise, requiring open communication and empathy. This combination is also associated with potential health issues affecting the spleen, pancreas, and gastric system, which can be managed through a healthy lifestyle. Despite challenges, the 4-2 combination offers opportunities for personal growth and spiritual exploration. In summary, it signifies a transformative journey of self-discovery, emphasising intellectual pursuits and the need for harmony within the family while promoting physical well-being.

4-3

The 4-3 flying star combination brings a vibrant and influential energy that impacts various aspects of life. It signifies intellectual pursuits, creative expression, and innovative thinking. Individuals may attract attention from women, but caution is advised. Women influenced by this combination may face mental disorders and emotional challenges, necessitating prioritisation of mental well-being. Additionally, the 4-3 combination carries the risk of deception, requiring vigilance in relationships and business dealings. Despite challenges, it offers opportunities for growth and innovation. By seeking support, maintaining awareness, and being discerning, individuals can navigate this combination and strive for personal and professional advancement.

4-4

The 4-4 flying star combination brings a favourable and auspicious energy that influences various aspects of life. It signifies academic achievements and success in exams, promoting recognition for intellectual abilities. This combination also supports romantic relationships and encourages adventure and travel. Overall, it signifies fame, success, and fulfillment in academics, romance, and travel. By embracing these opportunities, individuals can create a fulfilling life.

4-5

The 4-5 flying star combination presents health risks, including breast cancer and infectious diseases. It also warns against gang-related issues and the development of a gambling habit. It emphasizes the need for prioritising well-being, personal safety, and responsible decision-making. By taking proactive measures, individuals can mitigate risks and create a secure living environment.

4-6

The 4-6 flying star combination brings both positive and negative influences on life. It signifies potential financial success and fame, but also challenges in relationships, mental health, and physical well-being. It is important to approach relationships with care, seek support for mental health issues, and prioritise oral hygiene and safety. By addressing these challenges and seeking support, individuals can strive for a balanced and fulfilling life.

4-7

The 4-7 flying star combination brings challenging energy that can lead to conflicts, disharmony among women, legal disputes, potential injuries, loneliness, sibling rivalries, marital problems, and risks related to sexual matters. It is important to approach these issues with patience, understanding, and seeking appropriate support when needed to create a more harmonious and balanced environment.

4-8

The 4-8 flying star combination represents a powerful and transformative energy that brings opportunities for growth, success, and prosperity. It supports career advancements, financial gains, and recognition. However, challenges such as intense competition and power struggles may arise. It is important to remain focused, adaptable, and balance personal ambitions with relationship needs. By harnessing its positive energies and addressing challenges, individuals can maximise their potential for prosperity and fulfillment.

4-9

The 4-9 flying star combination represents a dynamic and influential energy that influences various aspects of life. It signifies intelligence, wisdom, and spiritual growth. This combination supports academic and professional pursuits, leading to a respected reputation. It also fosters creativity and original thinking. In some cases, it may be associated with diverse expressions of sexuality, including lesbianism. It is important to approach this aspect with sensitivity and respect. Overall, the 4-9 combination encourages intellectual growth, spiritual exploration, and respect for individual choices.

5-1

The 5-1 flying star combination brings forth negative influences that should be taken into consideration. It can lead to increased occurrences of inflammation in the bladder and various ailments related to the reproductive system. Additionally, diseases affecting the ears and potential hearing impairment may arise as well. It is important to be aware of these health risks associated with the 5-1 combination and take appropriate measures to prevent or address them.

5-2

The 5-2 flying star combination brings negative aspects that should be taken into consideration. It can result in the presence of widows and widowers within the household, indicating loss and sorrow. Additionally, an increase in stomach-related illnesses can be observed. In cases where this combination is coupled with unfavourable external features, it can potentially lead to significant calamities and, in severe instances, even fatalities. It is crucial to be mindful of these potential effects and take appropriate precautions to ensure the well-being and safety of individuals within the household.

5-3

The 5-3 flying star combination presents both positive and negative aspects. It signifies the potential for rapid wealth accumulation and high government positions. However, there is a risk of financial losses and accidents. It is important to manage finances wisely and prioritise safety. Overall, the 5-3 combination offers opportunities for success but requires caution and careful management.

5-4

The 5-4 flying star combination presents both health concerns and opportunities for success. It highlights the potential for health issues like breast cancer and viral diseases, emphasising the importance of regular check-ups and proactive healthcare. Individuals should exercise caution in risky endeavours like gambling to avoid significant financial losses. On the positive side, the combination supports women in business and those pursuing writing and academic success. By prioritising health, managing risks wisely, and embracing the supportive energies, individuals can navigate challenges and maximise their chances of achieving their goals.

5-5

The negative 5-5 flying star combination has detrimental effects on various aspects of life, especially outside the favourable period of period 5. It is associated with severe health issues, including the risk of coma, highlighting the importance of prioritising health and seeking medical attention when needed. During unfavourable periods, conflicts and hostility may arise, emphasising the need for caution, peaceful relations, and peaceful resolutions. This combination also poses risks of bone cancer, impotence, and physical injuries, requiring preventive measures and regular health screenings. By remaining vigilant about health, promoting peace and harmony, and taking necessary precautions, individuals can navigate the challenges and work towards well-being and tranquillity.

5-6

The 5-6 combination is linked to health concerns, including nervous system issues and mental health issues. It is important to prioritise self-care, seek support, and manage stress. This combination may lead to conflicts in relationships, so effective communication and patience are crucial. Financial challenges can arise, so caution and wise budgeting are advised. The 5-6 combination may create an unstable environment, so establishing stability and fostering a harmonious atmosphere is important. Despite these challenges, resilience, proactive measures, and balanced approaches can help overcome obstacles. Prioritising self-care, maintaining harmonious relationships, and practicing sound financial management can lead to a more stable and fulfilling life.

5-7

The 5-7 combination is associated with health concerns such as poisoning, venereal disease, and mouth cancer. Precautions and medical attention are important for individuals affected by this combination. It may lead to disharmony and conflicts in relationships, characterised by gossip and negative rumours. Open communication and healthy boundaries are crucial for minimising misunderstandings. The 5-7 combination can impact emotional well-being, necessitating self-care and support. Personal safety risks should be avoided through caution and mindful behaviour. Despite the challenges, awareness and proactive measures can mitigate negative outcomes. Prioritising health, cultivating harmonious relationships, and exercising caution lead to a healthier and more positive life.

5-8

The 5-8 combination supports loyalty to the government and brings prosperity. It is associated with wisdom and spiritual qualities. However, it carries the risk of betrayals and relationship difficulties. Maintaining open communication and healthy boundaries is important. Health concerns related to lungs and stomach may arise, particularly affecting young boys. Self-care and medical attention are crucial. The 5-8 combination can incline individuals towards sweet-talking and flirting. Integrity and consideration of consequences are important. Despite challenges, awareness and proactive measures lead to a balanced life.

5-9

The 5-9 represents an inauspicious combination where the 9 enhances the volatile 5 Yellow, making it more deadly. The presence of a 7 star can increase the risk of fires. This combination also affects health, particularly the eyes and the possibility of duodenal ulcers flaring up. Overall, the 5-9 combination brings both negative and positive energies. It can attract misfortune, accidents, and setbacks, requiring precautions. On the positive side, the 9 star represents future prosperity, growth, and favourable outcomes. Navigating the challenges while harnessing the positive energy is key for growth and prosperity.

6-1

The 6-1 combination is highly favourable for power, senior management, and politics. It signifies strength, authority, and financial success. It supports achievements in various fields, including sports and literature. Romantic opportunities are prevalent. Caution is advised in legal matters. Health risks include brain bleeding and injuries from sharp objects. The combination may weaken the father figure. By leveraging the positives and addressing the challenges, individuals can maximise the benefits of the 6-1 combination.

6-2

The 6-2 combination suggests extreme wealth and excellent health. It signifies a powerful family in the industrial sector, with financial gains from real estate ventures. Challenges include mental disturbances, one-sided love, and gastrointestinal issues. Caution is needed for reproductive and respiratory health. The combination attracts individuals inclined towards spirituality. Balancing the positives and addressing challenges maximises the benefits of the 6-2 combination.

6-3

The 6-3 combination signifies noble qualities and positions of authority. It brings government support and success in business and politics. Legal disputes and family conflicts may arise, requiring peaceful resolution. Health issues like headaches and accidental injuries are possible, so caution is advised. Financial inflow may come with challenges and physical limitations. Embracing the positives while being mindful of challenges can help navigate the 6-3 combination.

6-4

The 6-4 combination signifies financial success and recognition. It supports a comfortable lifestyle and fame through intelligence and academia. However, it may lead to extramarital affairs and marital strain. Females may experience persistent health problems, including eye and mouth ailments. Mental health issues and the risk of suicides should be addressed. Approach the 6-4 combination with caution, prioritise communication and self-care, and seek professional help when needed.

6-5

The 6-5 combination increases the risk of cancer and career difficulties. Prioritise health with regular check-ups and adaptability in the face of professional challenges. This combination is associated with headaches, lung cancer, and mental illnesses. Seek support for mental well-being and manage stress effectively. Be cautious in business ventures to avoid misfortune and seek professional advice. During waning periods, impotence and coma are possible risks. Prioritise overall health, seek medical guidance, and take necessary precautions. Despite the challenges, maintain a proactive mindset and seek guidance to navigate through difficulties.

6-6

The 6-6 combination supports careers, authority, and wealth. It offers government support and opportunities for military leaders and sports excellence. This combination signifies great wealth and recognition for scholars. However, it may involve lawsuits, family conflicts, and liver issues. Address challenges through cautious legal navigation, open communication, and proactive resolution of employee issues. Prioritise emotional well-being and promote a harmonious family environment. By managing challenges and harnessing the positive aspects, individuals can make the most of the 6-6 combination.

6-7

The 6-7 combination signifies political power, success in law, and sales skills. However, it also brings risks of robbery, conflicts among brothers, and relationship challenges. Precautions should be taken for personal safety, promoting open communication, and managing conflicts. Seek harmony and maintain a peaceful environment to navigate the challenges of the 6-7 combination.

6-8

The 6-8 combination brings success in real estate and good money luck. However, it can also lead to mental health challenges and negative influences. Prioritise mental well-being, avoid unethical activities, and seek support when needed. Approach the 6-8 combination with caution, focusing on personal growth, financial prudence, and maintaining a positive reputation to navigate its energies effectively.

6-9

The 6-9 combination brings potential riches, happiness, and success. It supports financial prosperity and recognition in fields like writing and government honours. However, challenges like rebellious behaviour, health issues, and sex scandals may arise. Exercise caution and balance to navigate this combination effectively. Prioritise personal and financial well-being, maintain family relationships, and take

care of physical and mental health to maximise positive energies and minimise negative influences.

7-1

The 7-1 combination benefits individuals with careers involving travel and exploration. It supports career growth through exposure to diverse opportunities. This combination also signifies a potential for romance, but caution is needed to maintain honesty and commitment within existing relationships. Embrace career opportunities and romantic connections while prioritising integrity and open communication. Navigate the 7-1 flying star combination for personal and professional fulfillment.

7-2

The 7-2 combination signifies financial prosperity and abundance. It supports economic stability and successful investments. However, it also brings challenges in relationships and emotions. Difficulties in conceiving and conflicts between family members may arise. It is important to address these emotional aspects and foster harmonious relationships. By promoting open communication and understanding, individuals can navigate the challenges of the 7-2 flying star combination while striving for both financial success and emotional well-being.

7-3

The 7-3 combination signifies financial success and supports business professionals, military achievements, and recognition in writing and literature. It also indicates potential gains through sports books and unexpected business profits. However, there are health and legal challenges associated with this combination. Poor health, hot tempers, and the risk of fraud and legal troubles may arise. Eye-related issues are also a concern. It is important to be cautious, seek legal advice, and take preventive measures to protect well-being and assets. By being proactive, individuals can maximise the positive aspects of the 7-3 flying star combination while mitigating potential negatives.

7-4

The 7-4 combination supports travel enthusiasts, offering opportunities to explore new places and cultures. However, there are health and legal challenges associated with this combination. Respiratory issues, such as constant coughing fits, may arise, requiring proper medical attention. Legal disputes and lawsuits are also possible, emphasising the need for caution and clear communication. By prioritising respiratory health and handling legal matters carefully, individuals can maximise the benefits of the 7-4 flying star combination while minimising potential obstacles.

7-5

The 7-5 combination is associated with health problems, including respiratory ailments and chronic conditions. Prioritising well-being, seeking medical care, and adopting a healthy lifestyle are crucial. Financial setbacks and instability may arise, necessitating caution, professional advice, and resource management. Emotional turmoil and anxiety are potential effects, highlighting the importance of self-care and seeking support. Conflict and disputes may occur, emphasising effective communication and peaceful resolutions. Navigating the 7-5 flying star combination requires resilience, proactive health management, financial prudence, emotional self-care, and conflict resolution skills to minimise its negative influences.

7-6

The presence of the 7-6 combination increases the likelihood of arguments and conflicts. Effective communication, patience, and understanding are important in mitigating these negative effects. This combination is also associated with a higher risk of skin-related diseases. Taking proper care of the skin and seeking medical attention when needed is advised. Tension and jealousy may arise, affecting relationships. Cultivating positivity, gratitude, and harmony can counteract these negative emotions. Navigating the challenges of the 7-6 flying star combination requires effective communication, skincare practices, and emotional management. Fostering a harmonious environment, practicing self-care, and maintaining positive relationships are key in mitigating its negative influences.

7-7

The presence of the 7-7 combination indicates an increased risk of fire hazards and armed robbery incidents. Caution, adherence to fire safety protocols, and security measures are crucial to minimise accidents and loss. There is also a higher probability of accidents, conflicts, and scandals. Prioritising personal safety, harmonious relationships, and ethical conduct is important. Superficiality in relationships and an increased risk of road accidents should be approached with attentiveness. The 7-7 combination suggests a higher likelihood of surgical operations and seduction situations. Prioritising health, seeking medical care, and maintaining fidelity are essential. Navigating the challenges of the 7-7 flying star combination requires caution, security measures, ethical conduct, and attentiveness to personal safety. Promoting a safe environment, open communication, and personal well-being mitigates its negative influences.

7-8

The 7-8 combination signifies auspicious financial opportunities that can be maximised with strategic planning and wise decision-making. Caution is advised to avoid risks and potential losses. It also creates favourable conditions for romance and relationships, emphasising the importance of honesty and open communication. While being aware of potential pitfalls and challenges, individuals can navigate them through prudent financial choices and nurturing healthy relationships. By prioritising emotional well-being and making the most of positive influences, the 7-8 flying star combination can be effectively managed.

7-9

The 7-9 combination signifies a powerful influence for innovation and progress, inspiring individuals with exceptional intelligence and creativity. It supports strong and fulfilling relationships, promoting love and commitment, and encourages activism for social justice. However, it is important to be aware of the negative influences, such as flirtatious behaviour and health risks. By channelling the positive energies, fostering healthy relationships, and taking necessary precautions, individuals can maximise the potential of the 7-9 flying star combination.

8-1

The 8-1 combination represents abundant wealth and prosperity, supporting financial success and a comfortable lifestyle. It bestows individuals with power, authority, and leadership qualities, aiding career advancement. This combination brings remarkable achievements, positive energy, and vitality. It also fosters a spiritual connection and appreciation for higher ideals. However, it is important to approach the 8-1 combination with wisdom and humility for sustained success and fulfillment.

8-2

The 8-2 combination signifies potential financial prosperity and abundance. It supports harmonious relationships and encourages creative expression. However, individuals should be mindful of potential health concerns and prioritise emotional balance. By practicing self-care and making wise decisions, individuals can maximise the positive aspects of the 8-2 combination and effectively navigate any challenges.

8-3

The 8-3 combination signifies a strong potential for intellectual growth, communication skills, and career success. However, individuals should be mindful of potential health concerns and prioritise emotional balance. Wise financial management is also advised. By focusing on personal growth, effective communication, and prudent financial decisions, individuals can maximise the benefits of the 8-3 combination while navigating any challenges that arise.

8-4

The 8-4 combination indicates favourable financial prospects and supports individuals in their pursuit of financial success. It encourages academic and artistic achievements while emphasising the importance of health and emotional stability. Family harmony is also highlighted. By adopting a balanced approach to finances, health, and relationships, individuals can maximise the benefits of the 8-4 combination while managing potential challenges.

8-5

The 8-5 combination brings financial instability and potential setbacks, as well as health risks, relationship conflicts, and career obstacles. Individuals influenced by this combination should exercise caution, prioritise well-being, maintain effective communication, persevere in their careers, and manage emotional turmoil. By adopting proactive measures and maintaining resilience, individuals can navigate the challenges associated with the 8-5 combination and work towards personal growth and success.

8-6

The 8-6 combination brings potential financial gains and creative abilities. It also indicates emotional sensitivity, relationship challenges, health concerns, and spiritual growth. Individuals influenced by this combination should seize financial opportunities, nurture their creativity, prioritise emotional well-being, practice effective communication, address health issues, and explore spiritual practices. By embracing the positive aspects and taking proactive measures, individuals can navigate the influences of the 8-6 combination for personal and financial well-being.

8-7

The 8-7 combination signifies conflicts, financial instability, health challenges, relationship struggles, emotional turmoil, and obstacles. Individuals influenced by this combination should practice effective communication, exercise caution in financial matters, prioritise self-care, foster understanding in relationships, manage emotional well-being, and maintain resilience. By implementing these strategies, individuals can navigate the challenges and strive for personal growth and resilience.

8-8

The 8-8 combination signifies prosperity, career advancement, personal power, positive relationships, personal growth, and favourable timing. Individuals influenced by this combination should seize opportunities, cultivate relationships, invest in personal development, and trust in the universe's abundance. By embracing these influences and utilizing their talents wisely, individuals can achieve significant success and enjoy a period of abundance and fulfillment.

8-9

The 8-9 combination represents a surge of creative energy and innovative thinking. Individuals influenced by this combination excel in artistic pursuits, technological advancements, and entrepreneurial ventures. They achieve success through determination and resilience, while also experiencing opportunities for wealth and abundance. This combination encourages spiritual growth and personal transformation, although challenges and obstacles may arise. By maintaining balance and adaptability, individuals can navigate this period successfully and unlock their full potential.

9-1

The 9-1 combination signifies ultimate success and achievement in various aspects of life. Individuals influenced by this combination reach the pinnacle of their endeavours, demonstrating strong leadership and authority. They experience career advancement, positive influence, wealth, positive relationships, and personal growth. This combination brings opportunities for recognition and prosperity, allowing individuals to inspire others and unlock their full potential. It is a time of great accomplishments and fulfillment.

9-2

The 9-2 combination signifies harmonious relationships and a nurturing environment. It supports educational and intellectual growth, financial stability, and the presence of supportive networks. However, it's important to note that there can be complications related to childbearing and gynaecological issues. This combination emphasises the importance of emotional well-being and radiates nurturing and compassionate energy. By seeking appropriate medical care and prioritising emotional balance, individuals can navigate these challenges and embrace personal growth and nurturing relationships.

9-3

The 9-3 combination signifies a creative and artistic potential, intellectual curiosity, and charismatic communication skills. However, it's important to note the potential for legal disputes and liver diseases. Individuals influenced by this combination should exercise integrity, seek legal guidance when need, and prioritise liver health. By doing so, they can embrace creative expression, intellectual growth, and responsible decision-making.

9-4

The 9-4 combination signifies academic excellence, leadership skills, and financial prosperity. However, it's important to be aware of the potential for unconventional relationship dynamics, abnormal sexual affairs, and incestuous relationships. Individuals influenced by this combination should prioritise healthy and respectful relationships, exercise discretion, and seek professional guidance when needed. By doing so, they can nurture fulfilling relationships while embracing their intellectual pursuits and financial goals.

9-5

The 9-5 combination fosters resilience and determination in individuals, but it can also lead to stubbornness and resistance to financial prosperity. Despite the challenges, those influenced by this combination can overcome obstacles by embracing adaptability and seeking support. Balancing stubbornness with openness to new ideas and collaborating with others can enhance personal growth and improve financial prospects. By actively working on these aspects, individuals can increase their chances of achieving success in various areas of life.

9-6

The 9-6 combination signifies potential health problems for individuals, particularly brain-related illnesses and lung diseases. To mitigate these risks, individuals should prioritise their well-being through regular check-ups, a healthy lifestyle, and proactive management of existing health conditions. Seeking medical attention promptly and adopting wellness practices can help improve overall health. Environmental considerations, such as ensuring good air quality, also play a role in mitigating the negative health effects. By taking these measures, individuals can work towards preserving their well-being and minimising the impact of the 9-6 combination.

9-7

The 9-7 combination signifies significant financial success and abundance, along with innovation and intelligence. However, it is important to be mindful of challenges related to relationships, fire hazards, health concerns, and reputation. Balancing social life and focusing on health are crucial. By taking proactive measures such as caution in relationships, safety precautions, maintaining a good reputation, and addressing health concerns, individuals can mitigate the negative impact of this combination. With mindfulness and responsibility, individuals can maximise the positive influences while minimising potential risks associated with the 9-7 combination.

9-8

When the 9-8 flying stars align, it brings happiness and fulfillment to romantic relationships. This combination fosters an abundance of love, memorable milestones, shared happiness, renewed passion, and joyful companionship. It is not limited to newlyweds or young couples but extends to older couples as well. The 9-8 combination also brings prosperity and success in partnerships. Embracing this positive energy creates a joyful and harmonious partnership filled with love and meaningful moments.

9-9

The 9-9 flying star combination signifies a fruitful period for the cosmetic and fashion industry. It brings financial abundance, creative expression, trendsetting influence, strong market demand, personal transformation, networking opportunities, and reputation enhancement. By embracing this positive energy, individuals can thrive and achieve long-term success in the beauty and fashion industry.

CHINESE ASTROLOGY IN PERIOD 9

CHINESE ASTROLOGY ZODIAC ANIMALS: MAXIMISING PERIOD 9 ATTRIBUTES

In Chinese astrology, the 12 zodiac animals play a significant role in understanding personality traits, compatibility, and life prospects. Each animal represents a specific period and possesses unique characteristics. To make the most of these attributes, it is important to embrace the strengths and navigate the challenges associated with each animal. By understanding the qualities and tendencies of your zodiac animal, you can harness its energy to enhance various aspects of your life, such as career, relationships, and personal growth. Let's delve into the wisdom of the Chinese zodiac animals and discover how to maximise their period attributes for a fulfilling and prosperous Period 9.

THE RAT
(1924, 1936, 1948, 1960, 1972, 1984, 1996, 2008, 2020, 2032)

The Rat is the first animal in the Chinese zodiac cycle and is associated with intelligence, resourcefulness, and adaptability. As we look ahead to the coming Period 9, which spans from 2024 to 2043, it is important to delve into the specific aspects of luck that the Rat may encounter during this period.

In terms of career and professional endeavours, the Rat can anticipate a promising outlook. The inherent intelligence and quick-thinking nature of the Rat will serve them well in navigating through the challenges and opportunities that lie ahead. Their ability to adapt to changing circumstances and think outside the box will give them a competitive edge in their chosen field. The Rat may find themselves presented with favourable opportunities for growth and advancement, as their hard work and determination are recognised by superiors and colleagues. However, it is important for Rats to remain focused and diligent in their pursuits, as periods of intense competition and unexpected obstacles may arise. By maintaining a proactive and strategic approach, Rats can maximise their chances of achieving success and reaching their career goals.

When it comes to financial matters, the Rat should exercise caution and prudence during Period 9. While there may be periods of financial stability and growth, there may also be times of unpredictability and volatility. Rats are advised to make wise decisions when it comes to investments and expenditures. Seeking expert advice or conducting thorough research before making significant financial commitments is recommended. It is crucial for Rats to maintain a balanced approach to money management, avoiding impulsive decisions that could lead to financial setbacks. By adopting a cautious yet proactive mindset, Rats can navigate the potential fluctuations in their financial circumstances and secure a stable future.

In matters of love and relationships, the Rat can expect a mixed bag of experiences during the Period 9. On one hand, Rats may have opportunities to form deep and meaningful connections with their partners. The Rat's intelligence and wit can be captivating, making them attractive to potential suitors. Those already in relationships may find that their bond strengthens as they navigate life's challenges together. However, it is important for Rats to strike a balance between their personal achievements and their commitment to their relationships. The ambitious nature of the Rat may sometimes cause them to prioritise their own goals over the emotional needs of their partner, leading to potential conflicts. By remaining attentive to open and honest communication, and demonstrating empathy and understanding, Rats can foster healthy and harmonious relationships.

The Rat's success in period 9 hinges on effective communication and embracing vulnerability. With their intelligence, adaptability, and strategic thinking, Rats can seize opportunities and tackle challenges across all aspects of life. By advancing their careers, overcoming financial obstacles, and nurturing meaningful relationships, Rats can lay the groundwork for a prosperous period. Despite potential uncertainties, their inherent qualities provide a solid foundation for success in this phase.

THE OX
(1925, 1937, 1949, 1961, 1973, 1985, 1997, 2009, 2021, 2033)

The Ox is the second animal in the Chinese zodiac cycle and is associated with reliability, diligence, and perseverance. Looking ahead to the coming Period 9, spanning from 2024 to 2043, it is essential to explore the potential luck and experiences that await the Ox during this time.

In terms of career and professional prospects, the Ox can expect a period of steady progress and growth. The Ox's strong work ethic, determination, and methodical approach to tasks will be highly valued in the workplace. They are likely to receive recognition for their reliability and ability to consistently deliver results. This period may present opportunities for the Ox to take on greater responsibilities and advance in their chosen field. However, it is crucial for the Ox to remain adaptable and open to new ideas, as changes in technology and industry trends may require them to update their skills and approaches. By embracing continuous learning and seizing opportunities for professional development, the Ox can enhance their chances of success in the ever-evolving professional landscape.

Financially, the Ox may experience stability and gradual growth during Period 9. The Ox's disciplined nature and cautious approach to money management can help them weather economic fluctuations and make prudent financial decisions. They are likely to prioritise long-term financial security and invest their resources wisely. However, it is advisable for the Ox to remain vigilant and avoid complacency, as unexpected expenses or market shifts may pose challenges. Seeking expert advice and diversifying investments can provide the Ox with a solid foundation for financial stability. With their patient and methodical mindset, the Ox can navigate the ups and downs of the economy and secure a comfortable financial future.

In matters of love and relationships, the Ox may experience stability and harmony during the Period 9. Their reliable and loyal nature makes them desirable partners, and they are likely to attract individuals who appreciate their steadfastness and commitment. For those already in relationships, the Ox's unwavering support and dedication to their loved ones will strengthen their bond. However, the Ox should be mindful of their tendency to be cautious and guarded emotionally, practice trust, faith and integrity and belief. With trust deep emotional connections can be experienced. By expressing their feelings openly and actively engaging in nurturing their relationships, the Ox can foster deeper intimacy and create a fulfilling romantic life.

The Ox's luck during the coming Period 9 promises gradual progress, stability, and opportunities for growth in various aspects of life. Their reliability, diligence, and methodical approach will be key assets in their career advancement and financial stability. By embracing change, remaining adaptable, and continuously learning, the Ox can stay ahead in their professional endeavours. Furthermore, by balancing caution with openness in matters of the heart, the Ox can cultivate lasting and meaningful relationships. The Period 9 holds great potential for the Ox to build a secure and fulfilling future by leveraging their inherent qualities and embracing the opportunities that come their way.

THE TIGER
(1926, 1938, 1950, 1962, 1974, 1986, 1998, 2010, 2022, 2034)

The Tiger is the third animal in the Chinese zodiac cycle and is associated with courage, passion, and independence. Looking ahead to the coming Period 9, spanning from 2024 to 2043, it is important to delve into the potential luck and experiences that await the Tiger during this period.

In terms of career and professional endeavours, the Tiger can expect a period of dynamic opportunities and challenges. The Tiger's natural charisma, leadership qualities, and competitive spirit may open doors to exciting new ventures and possibilities. Their boldness and fearlessness can propel them forward in their chosen field, allowing them to take on roles of authority and influence. However, it is important for Tigers to strike a balance between their assertiveness and diplomacy, as clashes and power struggles may arise. It is very important the Tiger shows respect towards others' opinions, boundaries, and preferences. By honing their communication and negotiation skills, Tigers can navigate these challenges and establish themselves as respected and influential figures in their professional domain.

Financially, the Tiger may experience a mix of highs and lows during Period 9. Their risk-taking nature and entrepreneurial spirit may lead to lucrative opportunities and financial gains. However, Tigers should exercise caution and avoid impulsive decisions that could result in financial setbacks. It is important for them to conduct thorough research, seek expert advice, and make informed investment choices. By maintaining a balanced approach and embracing a long-term financial strategy, the Tiger can overcome the potential volatility of the market and secure a stable financial future.

In matters of love and relationships, the Tiger may encounter a period of passion and intensity during Period 9. Tigers are likely to attract admirers with their magnetic personality and captivating charm. They may experience deep and passionate connections with romantic partners, filled with excitement and adventure. However, Tigers should be mindful of their impulsive nature, respect of opinions, boundaries and other preferences is imperative, plus settling themselves and the potential for restlessness in their relationships. It is important for Tigers to nurture open and honest communication, allowing their partners to feel secure and valued. By balancing their need for independence with a commitment to building meaningful connections, the Tiger can cultivate fulfilling and harmonious relationships.

The Tiger's luck during the coming Period 9 holds the promise of dynamic opportunities, challenges, and passionate experiences in various aspects of life. Their innate courage, charisma, and competitive spirit will be key assets in their professional pursuits. By navigating power dynamics with diplomacy and honing their communication skills, Tigers can establish themselves as influential figures in their respective fields. Financially, Tigers should exercise caution and make informed decisions to maximise their gains and minimise risks. In matters of the heart, Tigers can enjoy passionate and thrilling relationships by balancing their independence with emotional commitment. The Period 9 presents a fertile ground for the Tiger to showcase their strengths and create a future filled with excitement, success, and meaningful connections.

THE RABBIT
(1915, 1927, 1939, 1951, 1963, 1975, 1987, 1999, 2011, 2023, 2035)

The Rabbit or Hare is the fourth animal in the Chinese zodiac cycle and is associated with grace, compassion, and diplomacy. Looking ahead to the coming Period 9, which spans from 2024 to 2043, it is important to explore the potential luck and experiences that await the Rabbit during this period.

In terms of career and professional prospects, the Rabbit can expect a period of stability and steady progress. The Rabbit's natural diplomacy, attention to detail, and ability to work harmoniously with others will be highly valued in the workplace. They are likely to excel in roles that require strong interpersonal skills, such as customer service, counselling, or team management. The Rabbit's ability to create a peaceful and supportive work environment can lead to increased productivity and success. However, it is important for Rabbits to avoid becoming complacent and to seize opportunities for growth and advancement. By continuously developing their skills, staying updated with industry trends, and taking calculated risks, Rabbits can expand their professional horizons and achieve long-term success.

Financially, the Rabbit may experience a period of stability and moderate growth during Period 9. Their cautious and conservative approach to money management can help them navigate potential financial fluctuations and make prudent financial decisions. Rabbits are likely to prioritise financial security and focus on building a solid foundation for the future. However, they should remain vigilant and avoid unnecessary risks or impulsive spending. By maintaining a balanced approach and seeking expert advice when needed, Rabbits can make sound investments and secure a comfortable financial position.

In matters of love and relationships, the Rabbit can anticipate a period of harmony and emotional fulfillment during Period 9. Rabbits are known for their nurturing and compassionate nature, making them sought-after partners. They are likely to attract individuals who appreciate their gentle and caring demeanour. Existing relationships may deepen as Rabbits prioritise open communication, mutual respect, and emotional support. However, Rabbits should be mindful of their tendency to avoid conflict and suppress their own needs. It is important for them to assert themselves, express their desires, and maintain healthy boundaries. By fostering a balance between giving and receiving, Rabbits can create lasting and harmonious relationships.

The Rabbit's luck during the coming Period 9 holds the promise of stability, progress, and emotional fulfillment in various aspects of life. Their diplomatic skills, attention to detail, and compassionate nature will be valuable assets in their career and professional growth. By seizing opportunities for advancement and remaining open to continuous learning, Rabbits can achieve success and recognition. Financially, their conservative approach will contribute to stability and long-term security. In matters of the heart, Rabbits can foster loving and harmonious relationships by embracing open communication and asserting their own needs. The Period 9 presents an opportunity for the Rabbit to create a balanced and fulfilling future, leveraging their inherent qualities to thrive in all areas of life.

THE DRAGON
(1916, 1928, 1940, 1952, 1964, 1976, 1988, 2000, 2012, 2024, 2036)

The Dragon is the fifth animal in the Chinese zodiac cycle and is associated with power, charisma, and ambition. Looking ahead to the coming Period 9, which spans from 2024 to 2043, it is crucial to explore the potential luck and experiences that await the Dragon during this period.

In terms of career and professional endeavours, the Dragon can expect a period of significant opportunities and achievements. The Dragon's natural leadership abilities, creativity, and determination will propel them to new heights in their chosen field. They are likely to excel in positions of authority and influence, where they can make a substantial impact and leave a legacy. The Dragon's charismatic and influential nature will attract admirers and potential collaborators, creating a network of valuable connections. However, it is important for Dragons to balance their assertiveness with humility and respect for others' perspectives. By nurturing effective communication and teamwork, Dragons can foster a supportive environment that enhances their chances of success.

Financially, the Dragon may experience periods of both abundance and volatility during Period 9. Their ambitious nature and entrepreneurial spirit may lead to lucrative opportunities and financial gains. However, Dragons should be mindful of the potential risks associated with their bold investment decisions. It is important for them to exercise caution, conduct thorough research, and seek expert advice before making major financial commitments. By maintaining a diversified portfolio and being vigilant in monitoring market trends, Dragons can navigate the potential fluctuations and secure a stable financial future.

In matters of love and relationships, the Dragon can anticipate a period of passion and intensity during Period 9. Their magnetic personality and natural charm will attract potential romantic partners. The Dragon's passionate nature can create deep and transformative connections, filled with excitement and adventure. However, Dragons should be mindful of their tendency to be dominant and possessive in relationships. It is crucial for them to embrace open communication, respect their partner's values, goals, and individuality, and allow for mutual growth and independence. Shared projects will give a sense of alignment. By nurturing a healthy balance between passion and understanding, Dragons can build strong and fulfilling relationships that withstand the test of time.

The Dragon's luck during the coming Period 9 holds the promise of significant opportunities, financial gains, and passionate experiences in various aspects of life. Their leadership qualities, creativity, and ambition will be key factors in their career advancement and professional success. By fostering effective communication and collaboration, Dragons can create a positive and supportive work environment. Financially, Dragons should exercise caution and make informed decisions to maximise their gains. In matters of the heart, they can experience deep and transformative connections by embracing open communication and mutual growth. The Period 9 presents a fertile ground for the Dragon to showcase their strengths and create a future filled with achievement, prosperity, and meaningful relationships.

THE SNAKE
(1917, 1929, 1941, 1953, 1965, 1977, 1989, 2001, 2013, 2025, 2037)

The Snake is the sixth animal in the Chinese zodiac cycle and is associated with wisdom, intuition, and transformation. As we look ahead to the coming Period 9, spanning from 2024 to 2043, it is crucial to explore the potential luck and experiences that await the Snake during this period.

In terms of career and professional prospects, the Snake can anticipate a period of growth and transformation. The Snake's keen intuition, analytical skills, and ability to adapt to changing circumstances will serve them well in navigating the evolving professional landscape. They are likely to excel in roles that require strategic thinking, problem-solving, and a deep understanding of human nature. The Snake's ability to see beyond surface appearances and uncover hidden opportunities can lead to significant career advancements. However, it is important for Snakes to embrace flexibility and embrace change, as new technologies and industry trends may require them to update their skills. By remaining open to continuous learning and embracing innovation, Snakes can position themselves for success and thrive in their professional endeavours.

Financially, the Snake may experience a period of stability and potential growth during Period 9. As in Period 9, the Snake's Fire elemental nature gives it the support and strength needed, making money luck and financial gains appear promising. Their prudent nature, analytical thinking, and ability to make strategic financial decisions can help them navigate the economic landscape. Snakes are likely to prioritise long-term financial security and focus on building a solid foundation. However, it is important for them to remain cautious and avoid impulsive or risky investments. Conducting thorough research, seeking expert advice, and diversifying their portfolio can contribute to their financial stability. By adopting a balanced approach and staying vigilant, Snakes can maximise their financial opportunities and weather potential economic fluctuations.

In matters of love and relationships, the Snake can anticipate a period of deep emotional connections and personal growth during Period 9. Snakes are known for their wisdom, charm, and sensuality, making them attractive to potential partners. They may experience transformative relationships filled with intense emotional connections and profound understanding. However, Snakes should be mindful of their tendency to be secretive or overly cautious in matters of the heart. It is important for them to foster patience, understanding, open and honest communication, allowing their partners to feel valued and secure. By embracing vulnerability and expressing their emotions, Snakes can cultivate deep and lasting relationships that nurture their personal growth and bring them fulfillment.

The Snake's luck during the coming Period 9 promises opportunities for growth, transformation, and emotional fulfillment in various aspects of life. Their wisdom, intuition, and adaptability will be key assets in their career and professional endeavours. By embracing flexibility and staying open to continuous learning, Snakes can navigate the changing landscape and achieve success. Financially, their prudent and strategic approach will contribute to stability and long-term security. In matters of the heart, Snakes can experience profound emotional connections by embracing patience, understanding, open communication and vulnerability. The Period 9 presents a fertile ground for the Snake to showcase their strengths, achieve personal growth, and build a future filled with wisdom, prosperity, and meaningful relationships.

THE HORSE
(1918, 1930, 1942, 1954, 1966, 1978, 1990, 2002. 2014, 2026, 2038)

The Horse is the seventh animal in the Chinese zodiac cycle and is associated with energy, independence, and ambition. Looking ahead to the coming Period 9, spanning from 2024 to 2043, it is important to explore the potential luck and experiences that await the Horse during this period.

In terms of career and professional prospects, the Horse can anticipate a period of dynamic opportunities and progress. In Period 9, the Horse's Fire elemental nature gives it the support and strength needed, making money luck and financial gains appear promising. The Horse's natural enthusiasm, drive, and strong work ethic will propel them forward in their chosen field. They are likely to excel in roles that allow them to showcase their leadership abilities and take on new challenges. The Horse's independent and assertive nature will attract opportunities for career advancements, promotions, and recognition. However, it is crucial for Horses to strike a balance between their ambitious pursuits and maintaining work-life harmony. By prioritising self-care, setting boundaries, and nurturing healthy relationships, Horses can achieve sustainable success and fulfillment in their professional endeavours.

Financially, the Horse may experience a mix of opportunities and challenges during Period 9. Their enterprising spirit and risk-taking nature may lead to lucrative financial gains. However, Horses should exercise caution and conduct thorough research before making major investment decisions. It is important for them to strike a balance between seizing opportunities and managing risks. By seeking expert advice, diversifying their investments, and staying informed about market trends, Horses can maximise their financial potential and secure a stable future.

In matters of love and relationships, the Horse can anticipate a period of romantic adventures and emotional growth during Period 9. Horses are known for their magnetic charm, passion, and enthusiasm, making them attractive to potential partners. They may experience passionate and exciting relationships filled with adventure and shared experiences. Appreciation and expressions of gratitude towards there partner will garner great rewards. However, Horses should be mindful of their tendency to be restless and seek constant stimulation. It is important for them to nurture open and honest communication, and to cultivate emotional depth and stability in their relationships. By balancing their need for independence with commitment and emotional support, Horses can build lasting and fulfilling relationships.

The Horse's luck during the coming Period 9 holds the promise of dynamic opportunities, financial gains, and romantic adventures in various aspects of life. Their energy, ambition, and independence will be key factors in their career advancement and professional success. By maintaining a healthy work-life balance and nurturing personal relationships, Horses can achieve sustainable fulfillment. Financially, they should exercise caution and make informed decisions to maximise their gains. In matters of the heart, Horses can embrace passion and excitement while fostering emotional depth and stability. The Period 9 presents a fertile ground for the Horse to showcase their strengths, seize opportunities, and create a future filled with achievement, prosperity, and meaningful connections.

THE GOAT
(1919, 1931, 1943, 1955, 1967, 1979, 1991, 2003, 2015, 2027, 2039)

The Goat, or Sheep, is the eighth animal in the Chinese zodiac cycle and is associated with gentleness, creativity, and harmony. Looking ahead to the coming Period 9, which spans from 2024 to 2043, it is important to explore the potential luck and experiences that await the Goat during this period.

In terms of career and professional prospects, the Goat can expect a period of stability and gradual growth. The Goat's innate creativity, artistic talents, and gentle demeanour will be highly valued in fields such as art, design, music, or counselling. They are likely to thrive in environments that allow them to express their unique perspectives and foster harmonious relationships with colleagues. The Goat's ability to bring a sense of tranquillity and balance to their work can lead to increased productivity and a positive work atmosphere. However, it is important for Goats to overcome their tendency to be indecisive or overly cautious. By embracing their talents, trusting their instincts, and seeking opportunities for growth, Goats can unlock their full potential and achieve professional success.

Financially, the Goat may experience a period of moderate stability during Period 9. Their cautious and practical nature will contribute to their ability to manage their finances effectively. Goats are likely to prioritise financial security and make wise financial decisions. While they may not be prone to taking excessive risks, Goats should remain open to potential investment opportunities that align with their long-term goals. By maintaining a balanced approach and seeking expert advice when needed, Goats can navigate the financial landscape and secure a comfortable future.

In matters of love and relationships, the Goat can anticipate a period of emotional depth and connection during Period 9. Goats are known for their forgiving, nurturing and compassionate nature, making them highly desirable partners. They may experience loving and harmonious relationships, filled with mutual understanding and support. However, Goats should be mindful of their tendency to seek approval and avoid conflict. It is important for them to assert themselves, express their needs and desires, and maintain healthy boundaries. By fostering open communication and embracing vulnerability, Goats can create lasting and fulfilling relationships that nurture their emotional well-being.

The Goat's luck during the coming Period 9 holds the promise of stability, creativity, and emotional fulfillment in various aspects of life. Their artistic talents, gentle demeanour, and harmonious nature will be valuable assets in their career and professional growth. By embracing opportunities for personal and professional development, Goats can unlock their creative potential and achieve success. Financially, their cautious and practical approach will contribute to stability and long-term security. In matters of the heart, Goats can foster deep and meaningful connections by embracing open communication and asserting their own needs. The Period 9 presents an opportunity for the Goat to create a balanced and fulfilling future, leveraging their inherent qualities to thrive in all areas of life.

THE MONKEY
(1920, 1932, 1944, 1956, 1968, 1980, 1992, 2004, 2016, 2028, 2040)

The Monkey is the ninth animal in the Chinese zodiac cycle and is associated with intelligence, adaptability, and wit. Looking ahead to the coming Period 9, which spans from 2024 to 2043, it is important to explore the potential luck and experiences that await the Monkey during this period.

In terms of career and professional prospects, the Monkey can anticipate a period of exciting opportunities and intellectual growth. The Monkey's natural intelligence, quick thinking, and adaptability will be highly valued in a rapidly changing professional landscape. They are likely to excel in roles that require innovative problem-solving, creativity, and strategic thinking. The Monkey's ability to think outside the box and embrace new technologies will give them a competitive edge in the workplace. Additionally, their charismatic and persuasive nature can open doors to leadership positions and entrepreneurial endeavours. However, it is important for Monkeys to maintain focus and avoid being scattered in their pursuits. By setting clear goals, honing their skills, and maintaining a disciplined work ethic, Monkeys can make significant strides in their career and achieve professional success.

Financially, the Monkey may experience a period of both risks and rewards during Period 9. Their ability to adapt to changing circumstances and seize opportunities can lead to financial gains. Monkeys are likely to be drawn to entrepreneurial ventures and investments that offer the potential for high returns. However, they should exercise caution and conduct thorough research before making major financial decisions. It is important for Monkeys to balance their adventurous spirit with a rational approach to money management. By seeking expert advice, diversifying their investments, and maintaining a long-term perspective, Monkeys can navigate the financial landscape and secure a stable future.

In matters of love and relationships, the Monkey can anticipate a period of vibrant connections and intellectual stimulation during Period 9. Monkeys are known for their playful nature, wit, and charm, making them highly attractive to potential partners. They may experience relationships filled with laughter, shared interests, and intellectual compatibility. However, Monkeys should be mindful of their tendency to be restless or easily bored. It is important for them to cultivate deeper emotional connections by nurturing open communication and genuine support practically and emotionally, garnering more emotional intimacy. By embracing vulnerability and investing in meaningful connections, Monkeys can foster lasting and fulfilling relationships.

The Monkey's luck during the coming Period 9 holds the promise of exciting opportunities, intellectual growth, and vibrant relationships in various aspects of life. Their intelligence, adaptability, and wit will be key factors in their career advancement and professional success. By staying focused, embracing innovation, and honing their skills, Monkeys can achieve significant milestones. Financially, their ability to seize opportunities and manage risks will contribute to their potential for financial gains. In matters of the heart, Monkeys can cultivate vibrant and intellectually stimulating relationships by fostering open communication and emotional intimacy. The Period 9 presents a fertile ground for the Monkey to showcase their strengths, embrace new possibilities, and create a future filled with achievement, prosperity, and meaningful connections.

THE ROOSTER
(1921, 1933, 1945, 1957, 1969, 1981, 1993, 2005, 2017, 2029, 2041)

The Rooster is the tenth animal in the Chinese zodiac cycle and is associated with confidence, intelligence, and organisation. Looking ahead to the coming Period 9, which spans from 2024 to 2043, it is important to explore the potential luck and experiences that await the Rooster during this period.

In terms of career and professional prospects, the Rooster can anticipate a period of significant achievements and recognition. The Rooster's innate intelligence, meticulousness, and strong work ethic will propel them to new heights in their chosen field. They are likely to excel in roles that require attention to detail, organisational skills, and analytical thinking. The Rooster's ability to plan and execute strategies with precision will contribute to their success. Their confident and assertive nature will also help them thrive in leadership positions, where they can inspire and motivate their team members. However, it is important for Roosters to balance their perfectionism with flexibility and openness to new ideas. By fostering collaboration and embracing diverse perspectives, Roosters can create a supportive and productive work environment that enhances their chances of success.

Financially, the Rooster may experience a period of stability and financial growth during Period 9. Their meticulous nature and analytical thinking will contribute to their ability to manage their finances effectively. Roosters are likely to prioritise long-term financial security and make wise investment decisions. By conducting thorough research, diversifying their portfolio, and seeking expert advice when needed, Roosters can maximise their financial potential and build a solid foundation for the future.

In matters of love and relationships, the Rooster can anticipate a period of deep emotional connections and personal growth during Period 9. Roosters are known for their loyalty, honesty, and commitment, making them reliable and devoted partners. They may experience relationships built on trust, shared values, and mutual support. However, Roosters should be mindful of their tendency to be critical or overly judgmental. It is important for them to cultivate open and honest communication, and to embrace vulnerability in their relationships. By nurturing a supportive and understanding partnership, Roosters can create lasting and fulfilling connections that bring them emotional fulfillment.

The Rooster's luck during the coming Period 9 holds the promise of significant achievements, financial stability, and deep emotional connections in various aspects of life. Their confidence, intelligence, and meticulousness will be key assets in their career and professional growth. By balancing their perfectionism with openness to new ideas, Roosters can achieve success and inspire those around them. Financially, their strategic approach and wise investment decisions will contribute to stability and long-term security. In matters of the heart, Roosters can foster deep and meaningful relationships by embracing open communication and vulnerability. The Period 9 presents a fertile ground for the Rooster to showcase their strengths, achieve personal and professional growth, and build a future filled with accomplishment, prosperity, and meaningful connections.

THE DOG
(1922, 1934, 1946, 1958, 1970, 1982, 1994, 2006, 2018, 2030, 2042)

The Dog is the eleventh animal in the Chinese zodiac cycle and is associated with loyalty, honesty, and reliability. Looking ahead to the coming Period 9, which spans from 2024 to 2043, it is important to explore the potential luck and experiences that await the Dog during this period.

In terms of career and professional prospects, the Dog can anticipate a period of steady growth and fulfillment. The Dog's innate sense of loyalty, dedication, and strong work ethic will contribute to their success in the workplace. They are likely to excel in roles that require attention to detail, reliability, and teamwork. The Dog's ability to build strong relationships with colleagues and superiors will open doors to new opportunities and advancements. Their honesty and integrity will earn them the trust and respect of those around them. However, it is important for Dogs to step out of their comfort zone and embrace change and flexibility. By being open to new challenges and seeking professional development opportunities, Dogs can expand their skills and reach new heights in their careers.

Financially, the Dog may experience a period of stability and moderate growth during Period 9. Their cautious nature and practical approach to money management will contribute to their ability to handle their finances responsibly. Dogs are likely to prioritise long-term financial security and make sound investment decisions. While they may not be prone to taking big risks, Dogs should remain open to potential opportunities that align with their financial goals. By staying informed about market trends, seeking advice from experts, and maintaining a disciplined approach to saving and investing, Dogs can build a solid foundation for their future.

In matters of love and relationships, the Dog can anticipate a period of deep emotional connections and loyalty during Period 9. Dogs are known for their faithfulness, kindness, and protective nature, making them reliable and committed partners. They may experience relationships built on trust, mutual respect, and shared values. However, Dogs should be mindful of their tendency to worry or be overly critical. It is important for them to cultivate open and honest communication, and to embrace vulnerability in their relationships. By nurturing a supportive and understanding partnership, Dogs can create lasting and fulfilling connections that bring them emotional fulfillment.

The Dog's luck during the coming Period 9 holds the promise of steady growth, financial stability, and deep emotional connections in various aspects of life. Their loyalty, honesty, and reliability will be key attributes in their career and professional growth. By embracing new challenges and seeking professional development, Dogs can expand their skills and achieve success. Financially, their cautious approach and responsible money management will contribute to stability and long-term security. In matters of the heart, Dogs can foster deep and meaningful relationships by embracing open communication and vulnerability. The Period 9 presents a fertile ground for the Dog to showcase their strengths, build meaningful connections, and create a future filled with fulfillment, prosperity, and lasting relationships.

THE PIG
(1923, 1935, 1947, 1959, 1971, 1983
1995, 2007, 2019, 2031, 2043)

The Pig is the twelfth animal in the Chinese zodiac cycle, associated with generosity, kindness, and abundance. Looking ahead to the coming Period 9, which spans from 2024 to 2043, it is important to explore the potential luck and experiences that await the Pig during this period.

In terms of career and professional prospects, the Pig can anticipate a period of stability and growth. The Pig's innate traits of hard work, dedication, and loyalty will contribute to their success in the workplace. They are likely to excel in roles that require teamwork, collaboration, and problem-solving. The Pig's ability to foster harmonious relationships with colleagues and superiors will be highly valued. Their generous and compassionate nature will create a positive work environment and lead to opportunities for advancement. However, it is important for Pigs to maintain focus and avoid being overly complacent. By continuing to enhance their skills, embracing new technologies, and seeking out learning opportunities, Pigs can broaden their professional horizons and achieve long-term success.

Financially, the Pig may experience a period of moderate abundance and financial stability during Period 9. Their practicality, resourcefulness, and ability to save will contribute to their financial well-being. Pigs are likely to prioritise financial security and make wise financial decisions. They may have opportunities to increase their income through careful investments or additional sources of income. However, Pigs should remain cautious and avoid impulsive spending. By maintaining a balanced approach to money management, seeking expert advice when needed, and remaining disciplined in their financial habits, Pigs can enjoy a comfortable and secure financial future.

In matters of love and relationships, the Pig can anticipate a period of emotional fulfillment and harmonious connections during Period 9. Pigs are known for their caring, affectionate, and nurturing nature, making them highly desirable partners. They may experience relationships filled with love, support, and mutual understanding. Pigs are likely to prioritise their partner's well-being and create a loving and nurturing environment. However, Pigs should be mindful of their tendency to be overly trusting or naïve. It is important for them to maintain healthy boundaries, communicate openly, and assert their needs within the relationship. By nurturing strong emotional connections and embracing vulnerability, Pigs can create lasting and fulfilling relationships.

The Pig's luck during the coming Period 9 holds the promise of stability, growth, and emotional fulfillment in various aspects of life. Their hard work, dedication, and loyalty will be key factors in their career and professional growth. By remaining proactive, open to learning, and embracing opportunities, Pigs can achieve success and advancement. Financially, their practical approach to money management will contribute to stability and abundance. In matters of the heart, Pigs can cultivate loving and nurturing relationships by maintaining open communication and healthy boundaries. The Period 9 presents a fertile ground for the Pig to showcase their strengths, build meaningful connections, and create a future filled with prosperity, love, and contentment.

CAREER CHOICES IN PERIOD 9

Chinese Astrology Zodiac Animals: Favourable Career Choices in Period 9

The 12 Chinese zodiac animals hold valuable insights into career choices, particularly in Period 9. As we enter this period, it is beneficial to align our professional paths with the characteristics and strengths of our respective zodiac animals. By understanding the most favourable career choices for each animal in Period 9, we can make informed decisions and capitalise on opportunities for success. Whether you are a Rat, Ox, Tiger, Rabbit, Dragon, Snake, Horse, Goat, Monkey, Rooster, Dog, or Pig, unlocking the potential of your zodiac animal can lead to a fulfilling and prosperous career journey. Let's explore the career paths that resonate with the unique qualities of each zodiac animal in this auspicious period.

The **Rat** excels in careers that capitalise on their intelligence, adaptability, and strategic thinking. Period 9 best career choices for Rats are:

Finance
Accounting
Research

Consulting
Entrepreneurship
Law
Technology
Data analysis
Writing/editing

Their analytical mindset and attention to detail make them well-suited for roles that require problem-solving, financial acumen, and meticulous planning. Additionally, their strong communication skills can be an asset in positions that involve negotiation or client interaction.

The **Ox** excels in careers that require dedication, patience, and practicality.

Period 9 best career choices for Oxen are:

Engineering
Architecture
Farming or agriculture
Finance and banking
Project management
Skilled trades
Healthcare
Academia

Their strong work ethic and reliable nature make them well-suited for positions that require reliability and meticulous attention to detail.

The **Tiger** thrives in careers that allow them to showcase their boldness, leadership skills, and competitive nature.

Period 9 best career choices for Tigers are:

Sales
Marketing
Entrepreneurship
Sports
Entertainment
Public relations
Advertising
Journalism
The Arts

Their charismatic personality and ability to take risks make them well-suited for roles that involve creativity, innovation, and a dynamic environment.

The **Rabbit** flourishes in careers that utilise their diplomatic nature, creativity, and strong interpersonal skills.

Period 9 best career choices for Rabbits are:

Counselling or therapy
Human resources
Public relations
Event planning
Marketing
Writing/journalism
Design
Fashion
Hospitality
Customer service

Their ability to connect with others, maintain harmony, and bring a touch of elegance make them well-suited for roles that involve nurturing relationships, managing conflicts, and creating aesthetically pleasing experiences.

The **Dragon** thrives in careers that allow them to showcase their leadership abilities, ambition, and creativity.

Period 9 best career choices for Dragons are:

Entrepreneurship
Management
Executive positions
Marketing
Advertising
Entertainment
Public speaking
Politics
Design and innovation

Their charismatic personality, visionary thinking, and willingness to take calculated risks make them well-suited for roles that involve leading teams, driving change, and pursuing ambitious goals. Additionally, their ability to inspire others and think outside the box can be an asset in industries that require innovation and forward-thinking.

The **Snake** excels in careers that leverage their analytical thinking, strategic approach, and persuasive communication skills.

Period 9 best career choices for Snakes are:

Law
Finance
Consulting
Psychology
Research
Academia
Diplomacy
Sales
Marketing
Investigative journalism

Their ability to assess situations critically, make informed decisions, and navigate complexities make them well-suited for roles that require problem-solving, negotiation, and attention to detail. Additionally, their natural charisma and ability to influence others can be advantageous in positions that involve building relationships, managing conflicts, or presenting ideas effectively.

The **Horse** excels in careers that allow them to harness their energy, adaptability, and enthusiasm. Period 9 best career choices for Horses are:

Sales
Marketing
Public relations
Event planning
Hospitality
Travel and tourism
Sports and athletics
Teaching
Media and entertainment
Social work

Their natural charisma, sociability, and ability to work well under pressure make them well-suited for roles that involve networking, client interaction, and dynamic environments. Additionally, their strong sense of adventure and willingness to

take on new challenges can lead them to excel in professions that offer variety, excitement, and opportunities for personal growth.

The **Goat** thrives in careers that allow them to utilise their creativity, intuition, and compassionate nature.

Period 9 best career choices for Goats are:

Art and design
Writing and literature
Counselling or therapy
Psychology
Teaching
Social work
Healthcare
Hospitality
Nonprofit organisations

Their ability to connect with others on an emotional level, think outside the box, and bring a sense of harmony make them well-suited for roles that involve nurturing relationships, providing support, and promoting personal growth. Additionally, their artistic talents and keen eye for aesthetics can lead them to excel in industries that value beauty, creativity, and self-expression.

The **Monkey** excels in careers that allow them to showcase their intelligence, versatility, and charisma.

Period 9 best career choices for Monkeys are:

Entrepreneurship
Sales
Marketing
Advertising
Entertainment
Public speaking
Technology
Creative industries
Consulting and innovation

Their quick thinking, adaptability, and ability to think outside the box make them well-suited for roles that involve problem-solving, communication, and embracing new ideas. Additionally, their natural wit, charm, and ability to connect with others can be advantageous in positions that require networking, relationship building, and captivating audiences.

The **Rooster** excels in careers that allow them to utilize their organisational skills, attention to detail, and strong work ethic.

Period 9 best career choices for Roosters are:

Project management
Event planning
Administration
Accounting
Finance
Law
Research
Analysis
Writing/editing
Journalism
Public relations.

Their ability to plan meticulously, maintain order, and deliver high-quality work make them well-suited for roles that require precision, efficiency, and problem-solving. Additionally, their strong communication skills and sense of responsibility can be an asset in positions that involve leadership, coordination, and delivering accurate information to others.

The **Dog** excels in careers that allow them to showcase their loyalty, reliability, and strong sense of justice.

Period 9 best career choices for Dogs:

Law enforcement
Military service
Security
Social work
Counselling or therapy
Healthcare
Teaching
Customer service
Animal care

Their unwavering commitment to helping others, attention to detail, and ability to create a safe and supportive environment make them well-suited for roles that involve protecting, advocating for, or providing care to individuals or animals. Additionally, their strong sense of ethics and fairness can lead them to excel in positions that require upholding justice, resolving conflicts, and maintaining order.

The **Pig** thrives in careers that allow them to utilise their kindness, empathy, and strong work ethic. Period 9 best career choices for Pigs are:

Healthcare
Counselling or therapy
Social work
Teaching
Hospitality
Customer service
Event planning
Human resources
Nonprofit organisations

Their nurturing nature, ability to connect with others on an emotional level, and dedication make them well-suited for roles that involve caring for others, providing support, and creating meaningful experiences. Additionally, their attention to detail and willingness to go the extra mile can be advantageous in positions that require meticulousness, problem-solving, and ensuring the well-being of others.

GLOSSARY OF STANDARD TERMS AND MEANINGS

A

Annual star: A visiting yearly star to each of the eight palaces in every structure.

Auspicious: Something that is regarded as favourable, promising, or indicating a positive outcome. It implies good fortune, luck, or a propitious condition that bodes well for future events or endeavours.

B

Ba gua: An octagonal arrangement of the eight trigrams used as a basic tool of energy assessment in Feng Shui. Is often spelled as Pa Kua.

Ba gua Mirror: A flat, concave, or convex mirror surrounded by the eight trigrams and used to deflect negative energy or something in view that is not desirable.

Bazi: Is a Chinese astrology system also known as the Four Pillars of Destiny, meaning eight characters.

Black Hat Sect: Black Hat Sect Feng Shui is a form of Feng Shui created in 1980, practice that originated in Tibet and became popularised in the Western world. It focuses on the arrangement of the physical environment to enhance personal well-being and success. This approach incorporates various elements, such as furniture placement, colour schemes, and symbolic objects, to harmonise energy and promote positive influences in one's life. Most referred to as Ba gua Feng Shui.

Although not considered an authentic system of Feng Shui, Black Hat is one of the most recognised Feng Shui styles in the world except in Asian countries, which are more familiar with traditional schools of Feng Shui.

Black Tortoise: One of the four celestial animals, also known as the Four Guardians or Four Symbols. The Black Tortoise represents the northern direction and is associated with protection, support, and stability. It is believed to bring strength, resilience, and longevity to a space. The Black Tortoise is often symbolised by a tortoise or turtle, and its presence or representation in a home or office is believed to enhance the energy of the north sector and provide beneficial influences for the occupants.

Bright Hall: Is an open space near the front door (interior and exterior) where Chi can collect; in Chinese it is known as the Ming Tang.

C

Calendar, Solar: A calendar, like the standard Western one, based on the Earth's revolution round the Sun, but more precisely aligned to the seasons.

Cardinal directions: Points of geographic orientation-North, South, East and West. The specific and exact points of these directions are 0/360, North; 90 degrees, East; 180 degrees, South; and 270 degrees, West.

Celestial Animals: Green Dragon, White Tiger, Black Tortoise, Red Phoenix; these are essential landforms meant to support and protect the structure. It also ensures that Chi/energy may accumulate so that the occupants can thrive.

Central Palace: The location of the central stars of a chart and depicts the overall harmony of the chart. The Central Palace also refers to the pole star around which revolves the 28 constellations which mark the four seasons and the four animals.

Chi: The vital life-force energy of the universe and everything in it; sometimes Chi is referred to as cosmic breath. It is also spelled ch'i or Chi and is pronounced chee.

Chinese Compass: Also known as a Luo Pan, is a traditional compass used in Feng Shui and other practices in Chinese culture. It typically consists of a circular disc with concentric rings marked with Chinese characters, symbols, and directional indicators. The Chinese compass is used to determine the orientation, alignment, and energy flow within a space, providing valuable information for Feng Shui practitioners in assessing the Chi (energy).

Chinese Lunar and Solar Calendars: The ancient Chinese used the Solstices and Equinoxes to fix their calendar. 15° Aquarius is exactly halfway between the winter Solstice and the spring Equinox (on the Northern Hemisphere). This could be February 3, 4, 5. The Chinese chose the 15° Aquarius as the starting point of the spring season and the New Year. The spring Equinox falls exactly in the middle of the spring season; this is always on the 15th day of Mao/Rabbit month. Lunar calendar defines the lunar month on the first day of the appearance of the New Moon. A Lunar New Year begins on the 1st day of this new "moon". A lunar month is from the new moon to the next new moon. The ecliptic was divided into 12 equal divisions by the ancients. The Chinese Solar year is based on these 24 divisions called 24 solar terms. The year is divided into 24 Periods of 15 days.

Chinese New Year: The Chinese New Year occurs every year on the new moon of the first lunar month. The exact date can fall anytime between January 21st and February 21st. Each year is symbolised by one of 12 animals and one of five

elements, with the combinations of animals and elements cycling every 60 years. It is the most important Chinese holiday of the year. For Feng Shui purposes, the New Year begins on February 4th (based on the Solar Calendar).

Chinese Zodiac: Is a system that relates each year to an animal and its reputed attributes, according to a 12-year mathematical cycle.

Classical Feng Shui: Also known as Traditional Feng Shui. It is the authentic, genuine Feng Shui that has been developed and applied for hundreds, even thousands, of years in Asia.

Combination of 10: A wealth-producing chart in the Flying Star system where the stars add to ten in all nine palaces. Combination of 10 occurs in Period 9 SE 2/3 and NW 2/3 charts.

Compass School: Is a traditional approach to Feng Shui, emphasising the use of a compass, or Luo Pan, to analyse and assess the energy flow, or Chi, within a space. By determining the orientation and directional aspects of a building or site, Compass School Feng Shui aims to align the space with the natural elements and optimise the flow of energy for the well-being and harmony of its occupants.

D

Destructive Element Cycle: Refers to the relationship between the five elements (Wood, Fire, Earth, Metal, and Water) where one element weakens or destroys another in a cyclical manner. According to this concept, Wood consumes Earth, Fire melts Metal, Earth absorbs Water, Metal chops Wood, and Water extinguishes Fire. This cycle is used in Feng Shui to manage and balance the elemental energies within a space, promoting harmony and preventing excessive or detrimental interactions between the elements.

Direction: One of the 8 main compass points, or in a more specialised sense, the 24 Mountain ring. One of the most important aspects of determining the energy of a site or structure is taking the compass direction. Generally, the direction is read at the main door of the building or structure.

Door Facing: The facing direction of the door (generally of the front door).

Drain: An opening in the ground usually covered with a grate, which takes water away from an area. In Feng Shui, these are considered water exits and can bring wealth or disaster. A drain near a main door of a home or business is always bad.

Only exposed drains are important in Feng Shui; underground and invisible formations do not count.

E

Early Heaven Ba gua: Refers to one of the two primary arrangements of the eight trigrams in Chinese philosophy and Feng Shui. It is also known as the "Earlier Heaven" or "Heaven Sequence" Ba gua. In the Early Heaven Ba gua, the trigrams are arranged in a specific order that reflects the ideal or original state of harmony and balance. Each trigram represents a different aspect of life and is associated with specific elements, directions, and qualities. This arrangement is used in Feng Shui to analyse and harmonise the energy flow within a space, guiding the placement of objects and adjustments to optimise the positive influences and well-being of its occupants.

Earth Luck: One of the three categories of luck that humans can experience; your luck will increase by using Feng Shui, also known as Earth Luck.

Earth Plate: refers to a specific component found on the Luo Pan; the traditional Chinese compass used in Feng Shui. It is a circular plate or ring that is marked with various directional indicators and measurements. In particular, the Earth Plate is used to determine the directions and orientations of doors and buildings in relation to the compass directions. By aligning the Earth Plate with the desired reference point, such as the entrance or the main structure, Feng Shui practitioners can accurately measure and analyse the energy flow and adjust accordingly to enhance harmony and balance within the space.

Earthly Branch: Refers to one of the twelve animal signs used in the Chinese zodiac system. Each Earthly Branch represents a specific animal, such as the Rat, Ox, Tiger, and so on. These branches are associated with certain characteristics and traits that are believed to influence personality traits, compatibility, and fortune in Chinese astrology. The Earthly Branches are used to determine one's zodiac sign based on their birth year and play a significant role in Chinese culture and traditional practices.

As the Chinese Calendar is based on a combination of 10 Heavenly Stems and 12 Earthly Branches; there are 60 possible combinations equalling a cycle of 60 years. Earthly Branches are commonly known as the 12 Animal signs. When located on the 12 Earthly Branches ring of the Luo Pan, each Earthly Branch occupies 30°. When located around the 24 Mountains ring of the Luo Pan, each Earthly Branch occupies 15°.

Chen: The Dragon. One of the 24 Mountains located at 112.5° - 127.5°.

Chou: The Ox. One of the 24 Mountains located at 22.5° - 37.5°.

Hai: The Pig. One of the 24 Mountains located at 322.5° - 337.5°.

Mao: The Rabbit. One of the 24 Mountains located at 82.5° - 97.5°.

Shen: The Monkey. One of the 24 Mountains located at 232.5° - 247.5°.

Si: The Snake. One of the 24 Mountains located at 142.5° - 157.5°.

Wei: The Goat. One of the 24 Mountains located at 202.5° - 217.5°.

Wu: The Horse. One of the 24 Mountains located at 172.5° - 187.5°.

Xu: The Dog. One of the 24 Mountains located at 292.5° - 307.5°.

Yin: The Tiger. One of the 24 Mountains located at 52.5° - 67.5°.

You: The Rooster. One of the 24 Mountains located at 261.5° - 277.5°.

Zi: The Rat. One of the 24 Mountains located at 352.5° - 7.5°.

Eight Life Aspirations: Also known as the Eight Life Stations, these stations correspond to a point on the Ba gua and an aspect of life—South, fame; Southwest, marriage; Southeast, wealth; North, career; and so forth. Eight Life Stations is not found in classic texts. It is also not an aspect of the Eight Mansions system nor even a derivative of that system. But is very popular and used extensively by westerners.

Elements - Five: The Five Elements in Feng Shui, refer to the foundational elements—Wood, Fire, Earth, Metal, and Water—that are believed to interact and influence energy flow within a space. These elements symbolise different qualities, energies, and aspects of life, and their balance and harmonious arrangement are crucial for promoting positive Chi (energy), well-being, and harmony in each environment. The entire universe is energy; there are many types of Chi—human, environmental, and heaven (the solar system).

External environment: Refers to the surrounding physical features and structures that exist outside a specific location or property. It includes natural elements like mountains, water bodies, and the overall terrain, as well as human-made elements such as roads, pools, retaining walls, highways, poles, drains, washes, tall buildings, stop signs, fire hydrants, and other structures. The external environment plays a significant role in Feng Shui as it can impact the flow of energy (Chi) and influence the overall balance and harmony of a space.

Exhaustive Cycle of the Elements: Is the natural relationship and interaction between the five elements in Feng Shui. The cycle follows the order of Wood, Water, Metal, Earth, and Fire. In this cycle, each element can weaken or reduce the energy of the element that comes after it. For example, Wood can weaken Water, Water can weaken Fire, and so on. This exhaustive cycle is important in Feng Shui to maintain a harmonious balance of energies within a space and to address any imbalances or excessive energies that may be present. May also be referred to as the reductive cycle.

F

Facing Direction: The front side of the home or building, generally where the front or main door is located and faces the street.

Facing Star: Also referred to as the "Water Star," is a specific star located in the upper right-hand corner of each of the nine palaces or sectors in a Flying Star chart. In the practice of Feng Shui, the Facing Star is associated with wealth luck and is believed to influence financial prosperity and abundance within a space. It is considered an important factor to consider when analysing and optimising the energy flow and arrangements within a property to enhance wealth-related opportunities and outcomes.

Facing: The yang side of a building; this is important to establish in Flying Stars.

Feng Shui: Pronounced "fung schway". Means "wind water"; the two natural forces that drive Chi to a site. Feng Shui is an ancient Chinese practice that involves arranging and harmonising the physical environment to promote positive energy flow, balance, and well-being. It focuses on the placement of objects, furniture, colours, and other elements within a space to create a harmonious and supportive environment that can potentially enhance various aspects of life, including health, relationships, prosperity, and overall happiness.

Feng: The Chinese word for wind; pronounced fung, although foong is a more accurate sound.

Fire Burning Heaven's Gate: When the northwest location of your site, also known as "heaven's gate," has the presence of real fire, such as a stove or kitchen, it is referred to as "fire burning heaven's gate." This term applies specifically when the

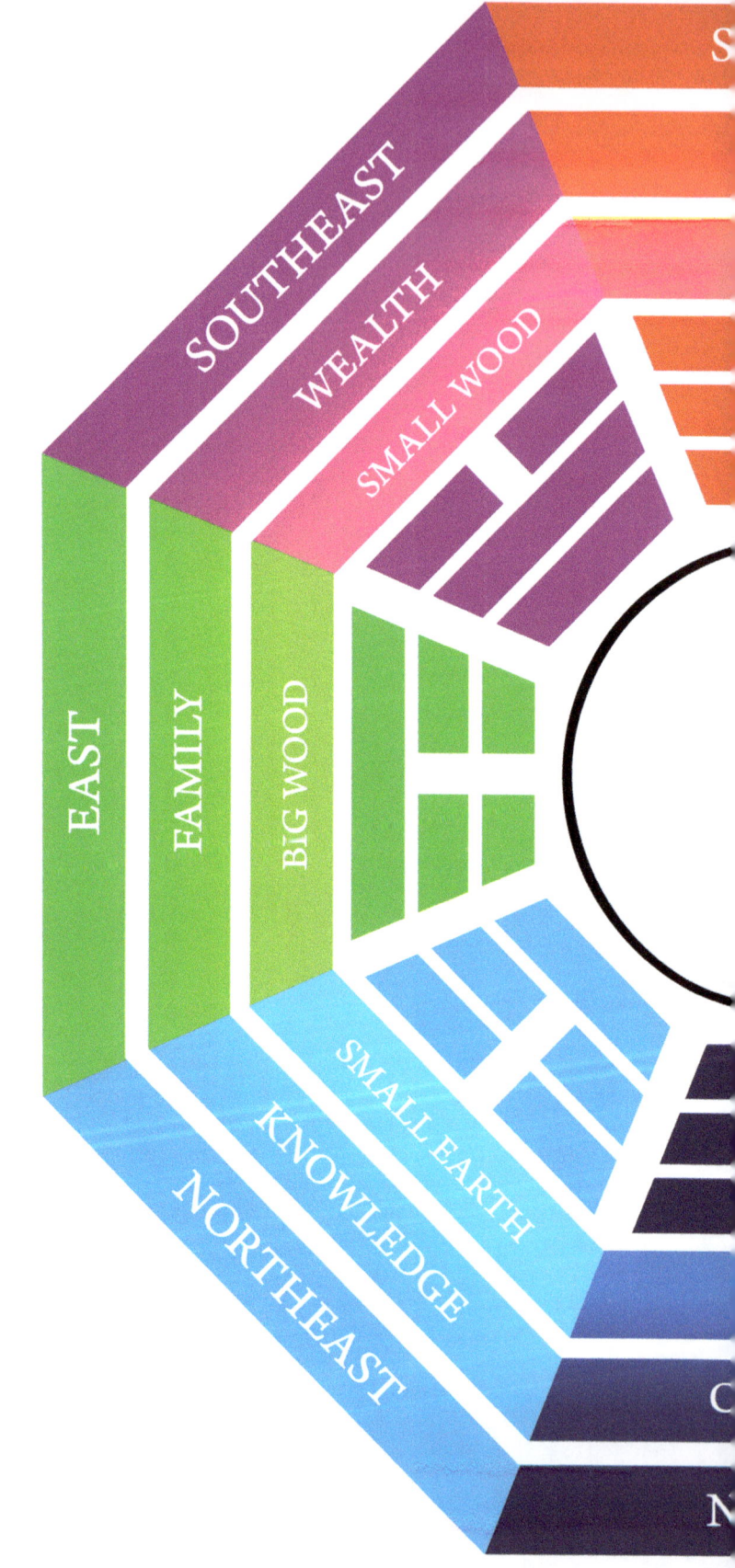

6 star (representing the heavens) and the 9 star (of the Flying Star system) come together in any palace, but it is considered particularly inauspicious when these stars align in the northwest palace. This combination of stars or the presence of actual fire in the northwest is believed to bring bad luck to the father, president, or leader.

Fire mouth: The direction of the stove knobs, a concept that is important in the Eight Mansions system. It is sometimes mistakenly referred to as the oven-mouth.

Five Chinese Metaphysical Arts: Are Mountain (Shan), Medicine (Yi), Divination (Po), Destiny (Ming), and Physiognomy/Imagery (Sow). Mountain encompasses philosophy, martial arts, healing, and Taoism. Medicine involves acupuncture, herbal prescriptions, and massage. Divination uses symbols and numbers for predictions. Destiny focuses on interpreting fate through astrology and fortune-telling methods. Physiognomy/Imagery predicts based on landscape, faces, architecture, and Feng Shui analyses the appearance, shape, and direction of a building.

Five Elements: Five types of Chi prevailing one after another (Wood, Fire, Earth, Metal, and Water) symbolise different energies and aspects of life. Balancing and harmonising these elements within a space is believed to promote positive energy flow, enhance well-being, and create a harmonious environment that supports various aspects of life such as health, relationships, and abundance.

Flying Stars: Known as Xuan Kong Fei Xing in Chinese is a sophisticated system that examines how time and space influence a building. It analyses the magnetic orientation and move-in date to determine the inherent characteristics of a house. It involves the study of subtle mysteries of time and space to understand the dynamic energy interactions within a structure.

Form School: Refers to the study of the shapes and physical structures in the environment, focusing on how they relate to the principles of the Five Elements. It involves analysing the forms of buildings, landscapes, and objects to assess their impact on energy flow and harmony. By considering the shapes and arrangements in relation to the Five Elements (Wood, Fire, Earth, Metal, and Water), Form School aims to create a harmonious and balanced environment that supports positive energy and well-being.

Four Pillars of Destiny: The "Four Pillars of Destiny" refers to your individual Chinese horoscope, which is determined by analysing the eight Chinese characters associated with your birth date and time. It involves examining the stem and branch of each component, including the year, month, day, and hour, to generate a comprehensive profile. This system is also known as Bazi and provides insights into your destiny based on the elements associated with each pillar of your birth chart.

G

Geomancy: A divination practice that involves interpreting the patterns and markings on the Earth's surface to gain insight into various aspects of life. It is based on the belief that the Earth contains hidden energies and influences that can be tapped into for guidance and understanding. Geomancy encompasses techniques such as dowsing, ley line mapping, and studying the alignments and arrangements of natural features like hills, rivers, and rocks. It is often used to assess and enhance the energetic qualities of a space, make predictions, and offer guidance in matters related to health, wealth, relationships, and other life concerns.

Geopathic Stress: Refers to harmful or negative energies that emanate from the Earth and can have detrimental effects on living organisms, including humans. These energies are believed to arise from various natural phenomena such as underground water veins, fault lines, and mineral deposits. Geopathic stress is associated with health problems, sleep disturbances, and overall well-being issues. Addressing and mitigating geopathic stress is important in creating a harmonious and balanced environment.

Great Cycle of 180 years: 9 cycles of 20 years. The current Great Cycle began 1864.

Green Dragon: The "Green Dragon" refers to the left-hand side of a property when standing at the front door and looking outwards. In traditional Feng Shui, this area symbolises the male aspect or energy.

Gua Number: Refers to a numerical value obtained through the calculation of an individual's birth date in Chinese Metaphysics, particularly in the practice of Feng Shui. This number is used to determine the individual's personal Gua, which represents their energy, personality traits, and auspicious directions for various purposes such as sleeping, working, or facing. The Gua Number is a key factor in Feng Shui analysis and recommendations for optimising harmony and balance in a person's environment.

Gua: Also spelled as "Kua," is a trigram representing one of the eight divisions in the Ba gua. It consists of a combination of three lines, either solid or broken, which form a unique symbol. Each Gua has its own symbolic meaning and associations, representing different aspects of life such as family, career, or health. The Gua's are utilised in various practices including Feng Shui and divination, providing insights

and guidance based on their individual characteristics and interactions within the Ba gua system.

Guest: Refers to a star that is treated as a visitor or guest by the host star in Feng Shui. It represents an energy or influence that enters a specific area or sector and interacts with the primary energy known as the host. The presence of the guest star can affect the dynamics and energy flow within that space, potentially influencing the overall balance and harmony. Understanding the interaction between the guest and host stars is important in Feng Shui analysis to optimise the positive influences and mitigate any potential conflicts or imbalances.

H

He Tu Diagram: A diagram that arranges numbers in specific positions, where 1 and 6 are in the north, 2 and 7 in the south, 3 and 8 in the east, 4 and 9 in the west, and 5 and 10 at the centre. This arrangement of numbers holds symbolic significance and is used in various Chinese metaphysical practices such as Feng Shui and astrology to analyse and interpret the relationships and interactions between different energies or aspects of life associated with these numbers and their corresponding directions.

Heaven Luck: One of the three categories of luck that humans can experience. The Chinese believe every human has a destiny and a fate determined by the heavens.

Heaven Plate: A ring found on the Luo Pan, a Feng Shui compass. It is used to measure the presence and location of real or virtual water within a space. This ring is also referred to as the "water ring" and plays a significant role in determining the energy flow and interactions related to water elements in each environment.

Heavenly Stem: In Feng Shui refers to one of the ten celestial stems used in Chinese astrology and Feng Shui practice. These stems are associated with the five elements (Wood, Fire, Earth, Metal, and Water) and are combined with the twelve earthly branches to form a 60-year cycle known as the sexagenary cycle. The Heavenly Stems are used in various calculations and analyses to determine auspicious and inauspicious energies, as well as to interpret and predict influences on different aspects of life such as health, relationships, and fortune. There are 60 possible combinations equalling a cycle of 60 years. When located around the 24 Mountains ring of the Luo Pan, each Heavenly Stem occupies 15°.

Bing: Yang Fire. One of the 24 Mountains located at 157.5° -172.5°.

Ding: Yin Fire. One of the 24 Mountains located at 187.5° - 202.5°.

Geng Yang Metal: One of the 24 Mountains located at 247.5° -261.5°.

Gui: Yin Water. One of the 24 Mountains located at 7.5° - 22.5°.

Ji: Yin Earth. Not one of the 24 Mountains. Located in the centre.

Jia: Yang Wood. One of the 24 Mountains located at 67.5° - 82.5°.

Ren: Yang Water. One of the 24 Mountains located at 337.5° -352.5°.

Wu: Yang Earth. Not one of the 24 Mountains. Located in the centre.

Xin: Yin Metal. One of the 24 Mountains located at 277.5° - 292.5°.

Yi: Yin Wood. One of the 24 Mountains located at 97.5° - 112.5°.

Hexagrams: The fundamental building blocks of the I Ching, consisting of 64 unique figures formed by combining two trigrams in all possible arrangements. Each hexagram is composed of eight lines stacked on top of one another, with each line represented as either broken or unbroken. These hexagrams serve as the foundation of the I Ching, a divination system and philosophical text, providing deep insights into the complexities of life and offering guidance and wisdom for decision-making, self-reflection, and understanding the natural and human world.

High-Rise Building: In the external environment, high-rise buildings and skyscrapers serve as man-made representations of mountains, playing a role like virtual or urban mountains.

Hsia: Pronounced as "she-ah", refers to the Chinese Solar Calendar that relies on the cycles of the Sun. This calendar is essential for agricultural purposes as it determines the seasons. It is also widely used in various Feng Shui techniques due to its precision. The solar year commences on either February 4th or 5th. The two possible dates exist not due to uncertainty but because of the Western calendar's slight irregularity caused by the inclusion of an extra day during leap years.

I

I Ching Feng Shui: Also called Xuan Kong Da Gua, is a Feng Shui system rooted in the I Ching's sixty-four hexagrams. Commonly known as the Big 64 Hexagrams, this approach provides a range of techniques, with auspicious date selection being one of the most popular applications. It is a San Yuan system that utilises the wisdom and symbolism of the I Ching to analyse and enhance the energetic aspects of

a space, offering insights and guidance for optimal energy flow and favourable outcomes.

I Ching: The I Ching, also referred to as the Book of Changes or Classic of Changes, is a profound philosophical and divinatory book rooted in Taoist mysticism. It consists of sixty-four hexagrams that hold symbolic meanings and interpretations. Dating back to around the 4th Century BC, the I Ching is attributed to four revered figures: Fu His, King Wen, the Duke of Chou, and Confucius. This ancient text serves as a guide for understanding the dynamic interplay of Yin and Yang, offering insights into the nature of change, balance, and the exploration of one's destiny and life path.

Imprisoned Ruling Star: The "Imprisoned Ruling Star" refers to the ruling facing star that is positioned or confined within the central palace. In Feng Shui, each sector or palace of a property has a specific facing star associated with it. When the ruling facing star is situated in the central palace, it is considered "imprisoned" or confined to that area. This positioning of the ruling star can have significant implications for the energy dynamics and influences within the space, potentially affecting various aspects of life associated with that specific star's characteristics and symbolism.

Intercardinal Directions: Northwest, Southwest, Northeast and Southeast.

Interior Environment: refers to everything contained within the confines of a structure, such as the kitchen, staircase, master bedroom, fireplaces, bathrooms, hallways, dining room, bedrooms, appliances, furniture, and other elements present inside the space. It encompasses all aspects of the indoor setting, including the layout, design, furnishings, and functional areas within a building or dwelling. Understanding and optimising the interior environment is crucial in Feng Shui to create a harmonious and supportive living or working space that promotes positive energy flow and well-being.

L

Later Heaven Ba gua: The "Later Heaven Ba gua" refers to the alternative arrangement of the trigrams. It is the second arrangement commonly utilised in the practice of Classical Feng Shui. This arrangement differs from the "Early Heaven Ba gua" and is extensively employed in various applications of Feng Shui, including the analysis and assessment of energy patterns, the interpretation of symbols, and the determination of auspicious and inauspicious influences within a space. The Later Heaven Ba gua provides a framework for understanding and harmonising the energetic dynamics in each environment.

Li Chun: Refers to the significant event of the commencement of spring in the Chinese calendar. It marks the day when the Annual Stars undergo a change, signifying the beginning of the Chinese Solar New Year. Li Chun occurs annually on February 4th, marking the start of a new cycle in the Chinese calendar. This date holds cultural and astrological importance, and it is often celebrated as a time of renewal and fresh beginnings. It is considered an auspicious time to set intentions, make plans, and align oneself with the energetic shifts of the new year.

Life Gua Number: Refers to the numerical assignment given to individuals in the Eight Mansions system (Bazi). It is determined based on a person's birthdate and gender. The Life Gua Number is used to analyse and understand the energetic characteristics and influences that shape an individual's life path and personal traits. This number is an essential component in Ba Zi astrology, offering insights into an individual's strengths, weaknesses, and compatibility with various aspects of life, such as career, relationships, health, and overall well-being. It serves as a foundational element in personal analysis and guidance within the Eight Mansions system.

Life Gua Characteristics: Refers to the descriptions of different characteristics, traits and personality types based on an individual's Life Gua number within the Eight Mansions system. Each Life Gua number corresponds to specific traits, characteristics, and tendencies that are believed to influence an individual's behaviour and preferences. These descriptions provide insights into how individuals with different Life Gua numbers may approach life, interact with others, and navigate various aspects of their personal and professional lives. Understanding your Life Gua characteristics can help individuals gain self-awareness, enhance their relationships, and make informed decisions aligned with their inherent traits and inclinations within the framework of the Eight Mansions system.

Location: Refers to a specific place or position within a given context, distinct from the concept of direction. It pertains to the physical placement or site of an object or area. For instance, in a residential setting, the living room may be situated on the south side of a home, indicating its location within the overall structure. On the other hand, the direction refers to the orientation or facing of an object or element within that location. In the example provided, although the living room's location is on the south side of the home, the desk within the living room is positioned to face north, indicating its direction. Understanding both location and direction is essential in Feng Shui for analysing and optimising the energy flow and arrangement of spaces to create a harmonious and balanced environment.

Luck: The composite result of three key factors: Heaven Luck (fate), Earth Luck (Feng Shui), and Man Luck (personal efforts).

Lunar Calendar: A calendar system that follows the patterns and cycles of the moon. It is determined by the phases of the moon, with each month typically corresponding to one lunar cycle. This calendar is widely used in various cultures and has significance in fields such as astrology, agriculture, religious observances, and cultural festivals. The lunar calendar differs from the commonly used Gregorian calendar, which is based on the solar year.

Luo Pan: is an essential instrument used by Feng Shui practitioners. It is a compass consisting of multiple concentric rings of information, typically ranging from four to forty rings. The most common design is a square wooden structure measuring around ten inches across. The circular part of the Luo Pan is made of brass and can rotate to align with the central compass. This tool is used to determine and interpret directional influences, energies, and other important Feng Shui aspects in each space.

Luo Shu: Refers to a square divided into nine palaces or sectors, each containing a numerical value that totals fifteen in any direction. This square, also known as the Magic Square of 15, is a fundamental component of Chinese divination and Feng Shui. It is also referred to as Luo River Writing or River Map. The Luo Shu provides a symbolic representation of cosmic principles and serves as a tool for various forms of numerological analysis, fortune-telling, and spatial arrangement. Its unique arrangement of numbers holds significance in understanding and harmonising the energetic influences within a space or in personal divination practices.

M

Magic Square: Also known as the Magic Square of Three and the Luo Shu. It is a square grid divided into sectors, where the sum of numbers in each sector, whether vertically, horizontally, or diagonally, adds up to 15. This mathematical arrangement holds symbolic significance in various fields, including mathematics, mysticism, and divination. The Magic Square represents a harmonious balance and order. Its properties are often used in numerology, fortune-telling, and Feng Shui to analyse and interpret energies, patterns, and influences in each context.

Main Door: The "main door" typically refers to the primary entrance of a home or business, often located at the front. In cases where occupants consistently use the garage entrance, that can also be considered as the main door.

Man, Luck: One of the three aspects of luck that individuals can encounter. It is the component of fortune that is influenced by personal actions and efforts. Man, Luck is characterised by factors such as hard work, dedication to study, educational pursuits, accumulated experience, and acts of kindness or virtue. Unlike Heaven Luck and Earth Luck, which are more external and uncontrollable, Man Luck is considered mutable and can be influenced and improved through individual choices and endeavours.

Man, Plate: A circular component on the Luo Pan, a compass used in Feng Shui practice. It serves as a tool to assess and measure the Chi, or energy, of mountains. By observing and analysing the qualities and characteristics of mountains, such as their shape, size, and placement, practitioners can gain insights into the energetic influences they exert on the surrounding environment. The Man Plate aids in the evaluation of these mountain energies, allowing for a more comprehensive understanding of the Feng Shui dynamics within a particular space or landscape.

Metal Cures: Remedial measures used in Feng Shui to counteract or weaken the negative influences of the Flying Stars 2 or 5. These stars are associated with challenging energies that can bring obstacles, misfortune, or health issues. The recommended metals for such cures include bronze, copper, brass, pewter, stainless steel, and wrought iron. By strategically placing or incorporating objects made from these metals in the affected areas, it is believed that the detrimental effects of the 2 or 5 stars can be mitigated or neutralised, promoting a more harmonious and balanced energy flow within the space.

Ming Tang: Refers to the "bright hall," which represents the courtyard or open space located in front of a building. It is considered a significant area where positive and beneficial Chi (energy) can gather and accumulate. The Ming Tang serves as an entry point for auspicious energy to enter a property, bringing good fortune and harmonious vibrations. By keeping this area clean, unobstructed, and well-maintained, it is believed that the flow of positive Chi can be optimised, creating a welcoming and prosperous environment for the occupants.

Ming: Refers to the concept of "life," "fate," or "destiny" in Feng Shui. It encompasses the understanding that everyone has a unique path and predetermined circumstances in life. Ming represents the combination of external factors such as birth date, time, and cosmic influences, as well as internal factors such as character, talents, and personal choices. It is believed that by understanding and aligning with one's Ming, individuals can make conscious decisions, cultivate positive energy, and navigate their life journey in a way that promotes personal growth, fulfillment, and overall well-being.

Monthly Stars: Refers to the transient energy influences that visit each of the eight palaces in Feng Shui. These stars represent the shifting energy patterns that occur monthly, bringing different qualities and influences on specific areas of a space. By understanding and analysing the effects of the Monthly Stars, practitioners can adjust and give recommendations to enhance or harmonise the energy in different areas of a building or property. This practice allows for the optimisation of the energetic flow and the creation of a favourable environment for the occupants.

Mountain Star: A specific star in the Flying Stars system that holds influence over health, relationships, and personality aspects. It represents the energetic force associated with mountains and carries significant implications for the well-being and interpersonal dynamics of individuals within a space. By analysing and addressing the Mountain Star in Feng Shui, practitioners can adjust promote harmony, balance, and positive energy flow in these crucial areas of life.

Mountains: In Feng Shui, "mountains" encompass both physical mountains and artificial representations, such as tall buildings, landscaped mounds, retaining walls, or large rocks. These elements hold significant influence over the energy flow and overall harmony of a space. Mountains are considered powerful symbols of stability, support, and protection. Their presence or absence can greatly impact the energy dynamics of an environment. By understanding and strategically working with mountains in Feng Shui, practitioners can optimise the energetic qualities of a space and create a more balanced and beneficial atmosphere.

N

Nine Stars: In Feng Shui, the "Nine Stars" refer to nine distinct types of energy, each represented by a number. These stars are considered living spirits that exert influence on various aspects of our lives. They play a significant role in different Feng Shui methods, including the Form School and Flying Stars. The Nine Stars are closely associated with the Big Dipper and Luo Shu, and are used to describe time intervals such as hours, days, months, and years, as well as units of 20, 60, and 180 years. In Chinese culture, these stars are also referred to as spirits. The practice of Nine Star timekeeping is primarily employed in Feng Shui for assessing and harmonising the energetic aspects of a space.

P

Pa Kua: Refers to the octagonal arrangement of the Eight trigrams, which are symbolic representations in Chinese cosmology. Each trigram consists of three lines, either solid or broken, and represents a combination of yin and yang energies. The Pa Kua is a fundamental concept in Feng Shui, used to analyse and interpret the energetic qualities and influences of a space. It serves as a key tool in understanding the interactions between different elements and energies in the environment for the purpose of harmonising and enhancing positive energy flow.

Pa Kua Mirror: A specially designed mirror that is encircled by the eight trigrams in the Former Heaven Sequence. It can be flat, concave, or convex in shape. The purpose of the mirror is to reflect and deflect sha ch'i, which refers to negative or harmful energy. The Pa Kua mirror is commonly used in Feng Shui to protect a space from adverse influences and create a more harmonious environment.

Palace: In Feng Shui, a "Palace" refers to one of the nine sectors into which a building is divided for analysis. Each Palace corresponds to one of the eight trigrams/directions, except for the Central Palace. Palaces are commonly identified by their trigram name or the compass direction they represent, such as the Li Palace or the South Palace. They serve as important areas of focus for assessing and optimising the energy flow within a space.

Parent String: The "parent string" refers to a specific arrangement of Flying Stars in a natal chart or a specific Period that holds significant importance in the practice. The parent string configuration consists of the numbers 1, 4, and 6 aligned consecutively within the Flying Star chart. This arrangement symbolises the nurturing and supportive energy of a parent, providing stability, protection, and guidance. The parent string formation is associated with the qualities of wisdom, authority, and strong foundations. It is believed to bring a sense of security, strength, and solid familial relationships to the occupants of a space. Activating and enhancing the parent string is thought to foster a harmonious and nurturing environment, promoting familial bonds, personal growth, and overall well-being. This configuration is highly valued in Feng Shui for its positive influence on family dynamics, stability, and emotional support within a home or workspace.

Pearl String: The "pearl string" refers to a specific configuration of Flying Stars in a natal chart or a specific Period. It is a highly auspicious arrangement that symbolises a string of precious pearls, representing abundance, prosperity, and good fortune. The pearl string formation occurs when the numbers 6, 7, 8, and 9 are arranged in a consecutive pattern within the Flying Star chart. This arrangement signifies a harmonious flow of positive energy, attracting wealth, success, and favourable opportunities. The pearl string is believed to bring forth a continuous stream of auspicious energy, enhancing the overall prosperity and abundance of a space. It is considered a highly desirable configuration in Feng Shui. Its activation and enhancement are sought after to harness its positive influences and support the occupants' financial well-being and success.

Period: Refers to a twenty-year cycle that has a significant impact on human luck and the energetic influences in the world. The observation and recording of these cycles' dates to approximately 2500 BC by ancient Chinese scholars. They discovered that every 180 years, the planets in our solar system align, and every twenty years, the shifting position of the Milky Way affects human affairs. The Periods are numbered from one to nine, repeating in a continuous cycle. Nine Periods form a larger cycle known as a megacycle, spanning 180 years.

Poison Arrow: A "poison arrow" refers to sharp or pointed objects, structures, or features that are directed towards a building or specific area. These objects or structures, such as sharp edges, corners, or tall structures, are believed to emit negative energy and disrupt the flow of positive energy (Chi) in a space. Poison arrows are considered inauspicious as they can create energetic imbalances and potentially impact the well-being, harmony, and fortune of the occupants. Feng Shui principles often recommend remedies or adjustments to mitigate the negative effects of poison arrows, such as using plants, mirrors, or screens to deflect or soften the harsh energy.

Productive Cycle: Refers to a harmonious cycle of creation and balance among the five elements. It is a cyclical relationship where each element supports and nourishes the next element in the sequence. The productive cycle is represented by the sequence of fire, earth, metal, water, and wood. Fire fuels the energy of earth, earth creates metal, metal holds water, water nourishes wood, and wood feeds the fire. This cycle symbolises the continuous flow of energy and the interdependence of the elements, promoting harmony and positive energy within a space. Understanding and applying the productive cycle is important in Feng Shui to optimise the energy balance and create a harmonious environment.

Prosperous Sitting and Facing: Refers to a specific Flying Star chart that signifies good fortune for individuals and financial prosperity. This chart is characterised by the ideal positioning of the auspicious stars, where the facing star is located at the facing direction (representing luck in wealth and opportunities) and the mountain star is situated at the sitting direction (symbolising support for personal well-being and relationships). The Prosperous Sitting and Facing chart is considered highly favourable as it aligns the positive energy of both the environment and the individual, enhancing the potential for success, abundance, and harmonious interactions.

Q

Qhi: In Feng Shui, "Chi" (pronounced "Chee") represents the fundamental essence and vital energy that permeates all aspects of existence. It encompasses both the tangible and intangible realms, serving as the life force that sustains and drives the growth, harmony, and interconnectedness of the universe, including the heavens, earth, and humanity. Qhi is often referred to as the breath of life, symbolising the essence that animates matter and energy in various forms. It is the unifying element that underlies the physical and metaphysical aspects of reality, encompassing the tangible substances and intangible energies that shape our surroundings and experiences.

Chi-mouth: Qhi, often referred to as "Chi" (pronounced "Chee") Refers to the entry point through which Qhi, the vital energy, flows into a space. It commonly refers to the front door of a building, as it serves as the primary gateway for Qhi to enter and circulate within the environment. The Qhi-mouth is considered significant as it influences the quality and flow of energy into the space, impacting the overall harmony and well-being of its occupants.

R

Red Phoenix: One of the four celestial animals, also known as the Four Guardians or Four Symbols. The Red Phoenix represents the southern direction and is associated with fame, recognition, and opportunities. It is believed to bring passion, vitality, and success to a space. The Red Phoenix is often symbolised by a mythical bird with vibrant red plumage. Its presence or representation in a home or office is believed to enhance the energy of the south sector and attract auspicious circumstances and positive outcomes for the occupants.

Reductive Cycle: The natural relationship and interaction between the five elements in Feng Shui. The cycle follows the order of Wood, Water, Metal, Earth, and Fire. In this cycle, each element can weaken or reduce the energy of the element that comes after it. For example, Wood can weaken Water, Water can weaken Fire, and so on. This reductive cycle is important in Feng Shui to maintain a harmonious balance of energies within a space and to address any imbalances or excessive energies that may be present. It can be referred to as the Exhaustive cycle of elements as well.

Retaining Walls: Tall structures, typically three to six feet high, that serve to stabilise and safeguard a site while preventing energy loss. These walls are particularly useful in landscapes with varying terrain or steep slopes. The purpose of retaining walls is to create a sense of stability and provide a barrier against any abrupt changes or potential energy drains in the environment. The number and placement of retaining walls may vary depending on the specific characteristics of the landscape, aiming to maintain a balanced and harmonious flow of energy throughout the space.

S

Secret Arrows: The harmful flow of energy caused by a direct alignment of roads, trees, poles, or neighbouring buildings. These straight alignments create a cutting effect on the flow of Chi, disrupting the harmonious energy in the environment. Secret arrows are considered negative influences that can create imbalances and affect the well-being of individuals living or working in such spaces. It is important to identify and address these secret arrows to redirect or mitigate their negative impact and promote a more harmonious energy flow.

Sector: Refers to a specific area within or around a building, such as the south sector, north sector, and others. These sectors are determined based on the cardinal directions or specific divisions of space. Each sector is associated with certain energies and aspects of life. Understanding and optimising the energy in each sector is an important aspect of Feng Shui practice.

Sexagenary Combinations: The 60 unique combinations created by pairing the 12 Earthly Branches (representing the animal zodiac signs) with the 10 Heavenly Stems (representing the five elements and yin/yang polarity). This system, also known as the Stem-Branch system, is an integral part of Chinese astrology and timekeeping. Each combination is associated with specific qualities and influences, and it is used for various purposes, such as determining auspicious dates, analysing personal traits, and predicting future events based on the interaction of the Earthly Branches and Heavenly Stems.

Sha Chi: Highly negative energy that is harmful and disruptive. It represents detrimental forces or "killing Chi" that can have adverse effects on your well-being and overall harmony. Sha Chi can originate from various sources such as sharp corners, cluttered spaces, pointed objects, or aggressive architectural features. It is important to identify and mitigate Sha Chi in your environment to promote positive energy flow and create a more harmonious living or working space.

Sitting: Refers to the back of the house or structure, symbolising its position as if it were sitting on the land or property. It represents the solid and grounding aspect of the house, like a mountain. The sitting direction plays a significant role in the energy flow and overall balance of a space.

Sitting Direction: Refers to the orientation or position of a house in relation to its surroundings. It is the opposite direction of the facing direction, indicating the side or direction where the back or supporting area of the house is located. The sitting direction plays a significant role in Feng Shui analysis as it influences the energy flow and interactions with the external environment.

Sitting Star: The Sitting Star, also referred to as the Mountain Star in the Flying Star system, has a significant impact on various aspects of people's luck. It influences factors such as fertility, employees, personality, and health. The energy associated with the Sitting Star plays a role in shaping the overall Feng Shui dynamics of a space.

Small Tai Ji: Refers to the central area of an individual room. It represents the core and focal point of the room's energy. The Small Tai Ji is an important element to consider in Feng Shui as it influences the overall balance and harmony within the space.

T

Ten Heavenly Stems: also known as the Ten Celestial Stems, are a system of symbols used in Chinese cosmology, astrology, and divination. Each stem represents a unique energy or quality and is associated with a specific element, direction, season, and other attributes. The Ten Heavenly Stems are Jia, Yi, Bing, Ding, Wu, Ji, Geng, Xin, Ren, and Gui. They provide a framework for understanding cycles, relationships, and patterns in various aspects of life, including time, nature, and human destiny. In combination with the Twelve Earthly Branches, the Ten Heavenly Stems form the basis of the sexagenary cycle, which is widely used in Chinese calendar systems and other traditional practices.

Ten Heavenly Stems

Jia (bud, signifying growth and potential),

Yi (sprout, representing the spreading of growth),

Bing (concentrated growth, symbolising fire),

Ding (maturity and solidity),

Wu (flourishing and nurturing),

Ji (full bloom),

Geng (harvesting and abundance),

Xin (transformation and renewal),

Ren (sustenance and support),

Gui (regeneration and preparation for spring).

These Stems are symbolic representations used in various aspects of Chinese culture, including astrology and traditional Chinese medicine.

Three Types of Luck: Also known as the Cosmic Trinity, encompasses the holistic understanding of a person's destiny and fortune. It involves the examination of three fundamental aspects: Heaven Luck, Earth Luck, and Human Luck. Heaven Luck refers to the cosmic influences and predetermined factors that shape an individual's life, such as their astrology and birth chart. Earth Luck pertains to the environmental and Feng Shui factors that surround a person, including the quality of their living or working space and its energetic flow. Lastly, Human Luck signifies the impact of personal choices, efforts, and actions in shaping one's own destiny. By considering the interplay of these three elements, a comprehensive understanding of an individual's overall luck and life journey can be gained in the practice of Feng Shui.

Tiger White: One of the four celestial animals, also known as the Four Guardians or Four Symbols. The White Tiger represents the western direction and is associated with strength, protection, and courage. It is believed to ward off negative energies and provide a sense of security and stability. The White Tiger is often symbolised by a powerful and majestic tiger. Its presence or representation in a space is believed to promote a sense of confidence, assertiveness, and resilience. It is considered beneficial to have the White Tiger energy balanced and harmonise d in the western sector of a home or office to create a supportive environment.

Tilting a Door: Tilting a door is a revered practice in Feng Shui, employed by experts and practitioners to alter the orientation of a door and influence the energy flow within a space. This technique involves adjusting the doorframe and threshold to align with a specific degree or angle of choice. By repositioning and rehanging the door accordingly, the energy dynamics of the area can be modified, creating a harmonious and auspicious environment.

Time Star: Also referred to as the Base Star in the Flying Star system, denotes the individual star positioned beneath the mountain and facing star within the chart. It holds significance in analysing the energetic influences and temporal aspects of a space. The Time Star plays a crucial role in determining the flow of energy and the manifestation of outcomes over time in relation to the other stars in the Flying Star system. Understanding and harnessing the power of the Time Star is vital for effective Feng Shui analysis and application.

T-Juncture: The configuration where two roads intersect at a right angle, resembling the shape of a "T". This formation holds potential negative implications when a home or business is situated at the top and centre of the T-juncture. The energy generated by this arrangement is considered unfavourable in Feng Shui, as it can lead to disruptive or challenging influences on the property.

Traditional Feng Shui: Synonymous term used to refer to Classical Chinese Feng Shui. It encompasses the ancient principles, methods, and techniques that have been practiced for centuries in the field of Feng Shui. Traditional Feng Shui focuses on the holistic approach of harmonising the environment, optimising energy flow, and creating balanced spaces to promote well-being, abundance, and auspiciousness. It involves the study and application of various systems, such as the Eight Mansions, Flying Stars, and Form School, to assess and enhance the energetic qualities of a space.

Trigram: Also known as a Gua or Kua, refers to one of the eight distinct symbols within the Ba gua. Each trigram is composed of a unique arrangement of three lines, which can be solid or broken. These trigrams hold symbolic meanings and represent different aspects of life and nature. The trigrams are integral to various Feng Shui systems and serve as a foundation for analysing energy patterns, determining auspicious directions, and understanding the interplay of elemental forces within a space.

Trigram Dui: Symbolising the marsh, it represents the youngest daughter and is associated with the element of metal. In the Xian Tian Ba gua, it is in the Southeast, while in the Hou Tian Ba gua, it is positioned in the West.

Trigram Gen: Representing the mountain, it symbolises the youngest son and is associated with the element of earth. In the Xian Tian Ba gua, it is in the Northwest, while in the Hou Tian Ba gua, it is found in the Northeast. It is also one of the 24 Mountains, positioned between 37.5° - 52.5°.

Trigram Kan: Representing water, it symbolises the middle son and is in the West in the Xian Tian Ba gua, and in the North in the Hou Tian Ba gua.

Trigram Kun: Symbolising earth, it represents the mother and is in the North in the Xian Tian Ba gua, and in the Southwest in the Hou Tian Ba gua. It is also one of the 24 Mountains, positioned between 217.5° - 232.5°.

Trigram Li: Symbolising fire, it represents the middle daughter and is associated with the element of fire. It is in the East in the Xian Tian Ba gua, and in the South in the Hou Tian Ba gua.

Trigram Qian: Representing heaven, it symbolises the father and is associated with the element of metal. It is in the South in the Xian Tian Ba gua, and in the Northwest in the Hou Tian Ba gua. It is also one of the 24 Mountains, positioned between 307.5° - 322.5°.

Trigram Xun: Symbolising wind, it represents the eldest daughter and is associated with the element of wood. It is in the Southwest in the Xian Tian Ba gua, and in the Southeast in the Hou Tian Ba gua. It is also one of the 24 Mountains, positioned between 127.5° - 142.5°.

Trigram Zhen: Symbolising thunder, it represents the eldest son and is associated with the element of wood. It is in the Northeast in the Xian Tian Ba gua, and in the East in the Hou Tian Ba gua.

Twelve Animals: Encompass the Rat, Ox, Tiger, Rabbit, Dragon, Snake, Horse, Goat, Monkey, Rooster, Dog, and Pig. They hold significant importance in the Chinese Zodiac and play a crucial role in Classical Feng Shui and Chinese Astrology.

Twelve Earthy Branches

Tzi (Rat),

Chou (Ox),

Yin (Tiger),

Mao (Rabbit),

Chen (Dragon),

Su (Snake),

Wu (Horse),

Wei (Goat),

Shen (Monkey)

You (Rooster),

Xu (Dog),

Hai (Pig).

Twenty-four Mountains: Represents the various facing directions of a structure, divided into 15-degree increments to form 24 directions. They are not actual mountains but serve as key references in Feng Shui analysis. Each Luo pan typically includes a ring indicating the 24 mountains. The 24 mountains are utilised in Feng Shui to evaluate the surroundings and the structure.

V

Virtual Mountains: Refers to tall structures like apartments, office buildings, and skyscrapers that are considered as substitutes for natural mountains in urban environments. These man-made structures possess a similar influence on the energy of surrounding buildings, affecting the Feng Shui dynamics of the area.

Virtual Water: Virtual water refers to man-made features such as roads, sidewalks, driveways, highways, and other formations that serve as conduits for the flow of Chi energy. These artificial pathways mimic the characteristics of natural water in Feng Shui, influencing the movement and distribution of energy within a given space.

W

Water: Water is a vital element in Feng Shui, holding the key to unlocking abundance, prosperity, longevity, noble connections, and harmonious relationships. Referred to as "Shui" in Chinese, it symbolises the flow of energy and life force. Within the realm of Feng Shui, water is recognised as the most potent and influential element, exerting a profound impact on the energy dynamics of the environment.

Water Star: The Water Star, also known as the Facing Star in the Flying Star system, governs the aspects of wealth luck. It holds the power to influence the financial fortunes and abundance within a space.

Waterfalls: Utilised in Feng Shui to amplify and attract wealth luck, with the direction of the waterfall playing a crucial role in its effectiveness.

White Tiger: One of the four celestial animals, also known as the Four Guardians or Four Symbols. The White Tiger represents the western direction and is associated with strength, protection, and courage. It is believed to ward off negative energies and provide a sense of security and stability. The White Tiger is often symbolised by a powerful and majestic tiger. Its presence or representation in a space is believed to promote a sense of confidence, assertiveness, and resilience. It is considered beneficial to have the White Tiger energy balanced and harmonise d in the western sector of a home or office to create a supportive environment.

Y

Yang: Refers to vibrant and dynamic energy, embodying the active and masculine qualities within the Yin-Yang symbol. It signifies the lively forces observed in nature, such as light, heat, and aridity. In human terms, yang symbolises masculinity and the optimistic aspects of our emotions. Furthermore, yang represents the realm of existence and vitality.

Yin-Yang Symbol: Also known as the Tai Chi symbol, is a fundamental concept in Chinese philosophy and represents the interplay and balance between opposing forces. It consists of two halves, one black (Yin) and one white (Yang), with a small dot of each colour within the other's domain. Yin represents the feminine, passive, and receptive aspects, while Yang represents the masculine, active, and assertive aspects. The symbol illustrates the harmonious coexistence and interdependence of these contrasting forces, as well as their continuous transformation and the potential for one to transform into the other. It embodies the idea of duality and the interconnectedness of seemingly opposing elements in the natural world.

Yin: Energy, often associated with femininity, represents the passive and receptive aspects of nature and life. It is the counterpart to yang energy, forming a harmonious balance. Yin is characterised by qualities such as darkness, coldness, and moisture. In human terms, yin symbolises femininity, stillness, and introspection. It also represents the realm of the deceased or the spiritual realm. Together, yin and yang form a dynamic interplay, reflecting the dualistic nature of existence and the interconnectedness of opposing forces.

Z

Zen: The concept of Zen refers to creating a harmonious and balanced environment that promotes peace, serenity, and a sense of tranquillity. It emphasises simplicity, minimalism, and the elimination of clutter to allow for the free flow of energy (Chi) and create a peaceful atmosphere. Incorporating Zen principles in Feng Shui involves creating clean and uncluttered spaces, using natural materials, incorporating soothing colours, and fostering a sense of mindfulness and presence in the surroundings. The goal is to create a space that supports relaxation, clarity of mind, and a deeper connection with one's inner self.

BEGINNERS FENG SHUI

'EASY TIPS TO ENHANCE EVERYDAY LIVING'

A beginner's guide to learning the fundamentals of Feng Shui and energy flow in the home, known as Chi. This ancient art of placement brings balance, helps to improve the harmony and prosperity within your space. Ideal as a gift for the novice wanting to learn more or beautiful coffee table book to inspire you on your next home renovation.

Buy Beginners Feng Shui   www.completefengshui.com

Ebook Beginners Feng Shui   www.completefengshui.com

COMPLETE FENG SHUI NEWS IS FOR YOU - TO NAVIGATE AND UNDERSTAND YOURSELF AND ENVIRONMENT:

MONTHLY SUBSCRIPTION

- Monthly Feng Shui and Flying Star Outlook
- All 12 Animals Chinese Horoscope Forecasts and Day Masters
- Calendar Auspicious date selection… And much, much more
- Over 40 pages to navigate monthly Feng Shui

Subscribe   www.completefengshui.com

COURSES / WORKSHOPS

- Complete Lifestyle Retreat
- Understanding Feng Shui and your home
- Landform and Symbolism… making the most of your home and interior
- Show Me the Money – Chinese Astrology for Career, Wealth and Success
- Lifestyle Feng Shui – Better Living with Feng Shui
- Good Feng Shui… Property and Real Estate
- Getting to Know YOU, Beginners Chinese Astrology Part 1 & 2
- Module 1: Health, Wealth & Prosperity
- Module 2: Four Pillars of Destiny Part 1 & 2
- Module 3: Flying Stars Part 1 & 2
- Module 4: Practitioners Course and Business Practices for a Feng Shui Business
- Feng Shui Refresher workshop

ABOUT MICHELE CASTLE

Michele has been in demand as a Feng Shui consultant for nearly two decades. Trained by Master Raymond Lo of Hong Kong, at the Juliana Abraham Feng Shui Centre in Perth, Western Australia, and has studied with Dato Joey Yap and Lillian Too. Michele maintains her Master studies each year to ensure she continues to provide clients with the best of her skills. Michele has an uncanny ability to read charts and has a fantastic insight into people. She combines experience and natural intuition with the multi-layered discipline of Feng Shui, to deliver positive outcomes for clients. Michele's approach is practical, realistic and simple. She adores the reward of making a difference in the lives of her valued clients.

Having studied architectural drafting and interior design and working with interiors and renovations on her own homes it was a natural progression to incorporate Feng Shui and metaphysical studies into those projects. Applauded for her style, Michele was often asked if she could share her gift with others. Passion and dedication, combined with further studies, saw her first Feng Shui business, Energize Life Feng Shui born and evolve into Complete Feng Shui.

Michele conducts onsite Feng Shui consultations for residential and corporate clients. An accredited teacher, at recognised training institutes, author and public speaker with numerous radio and television guest appearances. Michele works alongside families, with residential homes, developers, architects, interior designers, real estate agents, restaurants, cafes, day spas and retail stores.

For any existing or proposed business client Michele can help with staff recruitment, choosing the best location and orientation for business premises, improving the atmosphere, and working environment, and advisement on business stationery such as letterheads and business cards.

For the residential client, Michele offers guidance on how to improve health and harmony in the home, how to choose the best home for you and how to improve the chances of selling your home. Other services include how to choose a suitable career for children or elderly family members and how to improve children's behavior, sleep, and studies.

Michele's practice and qualifications include Classical, Form, Ba gua, 8 Mansions, 24 Mountain Compass, Flying Star School Feng Shui, site selection and design. Metaphysical studies of Four Pillars of Destiny / Bazi / Pa Chee, Qi Men, Millionaires Feng Shui with special interest and studies on Feng Shui Love and relationship luck.

Michele teaches beginner to practitioner Feng Shui seminars, workshops, courses, and retreats, as well as conducting on-site learning experiences at homes and businesses. Students receive complete course notes. For those who have mastered the basics of Feng Shui and wish to continue their studies and share their knowledge with others, there are courses to explore.

With an ability to relate to people from all walks of life. Based in Perth, but regularly consulting in UK, South Africa, Malaysia, Singapore, Bali and eastern states of Australia on residential, business, and commercial properties.

AUTHOR

Beginners Feng Shui - Easy Tips to Enhance Everyday Life.
365 Everyday Feng Shui Tips Journal
Complete Feng Shui Monthly Planner 2022
Complete Feng Shui Diary 2022 - Year of Water Tiger
2022 Year of Water Tiger Feng Shui and Chinese Astrology
2023 Year of Water Rabbit Feng Shui and Chinese Astrology
Michele truly believes, "Life is what our thoughts environment and energy make it". "Change your environment and thoughts, change your life".

With the knowledge of Feng Shui, it can work to increase wealth, enhance health, and harmonise relationships.

BEGINNERS FENG SHUI 'EASY TIPS TO ENHANCE EVERYDAY LIVING'

A beginner's guide to learning the fundamentals of Feng Shui and energy flow in the home, known as Chi. This ancient art of placement which brings balance, helps to improve the harmony and prosperity within your space. Ideal as a gift for the novice wanting to learn more or beautiful coffee table book to inspire you on your next home renovation.

Beginners Feng Shui www.completefengshui.com

365 EVERYDAY TIPS JOURNAL 'EASY TIPS TO FOLLOW TO ENHANCE EVERYDAY LIFE'

www.completefengshui.com

www.ingramcontent.com/pod-product-compliance
Lightning Source LLC
Chambersburg PA
CBHW061131010526
44107CB00068B/2907